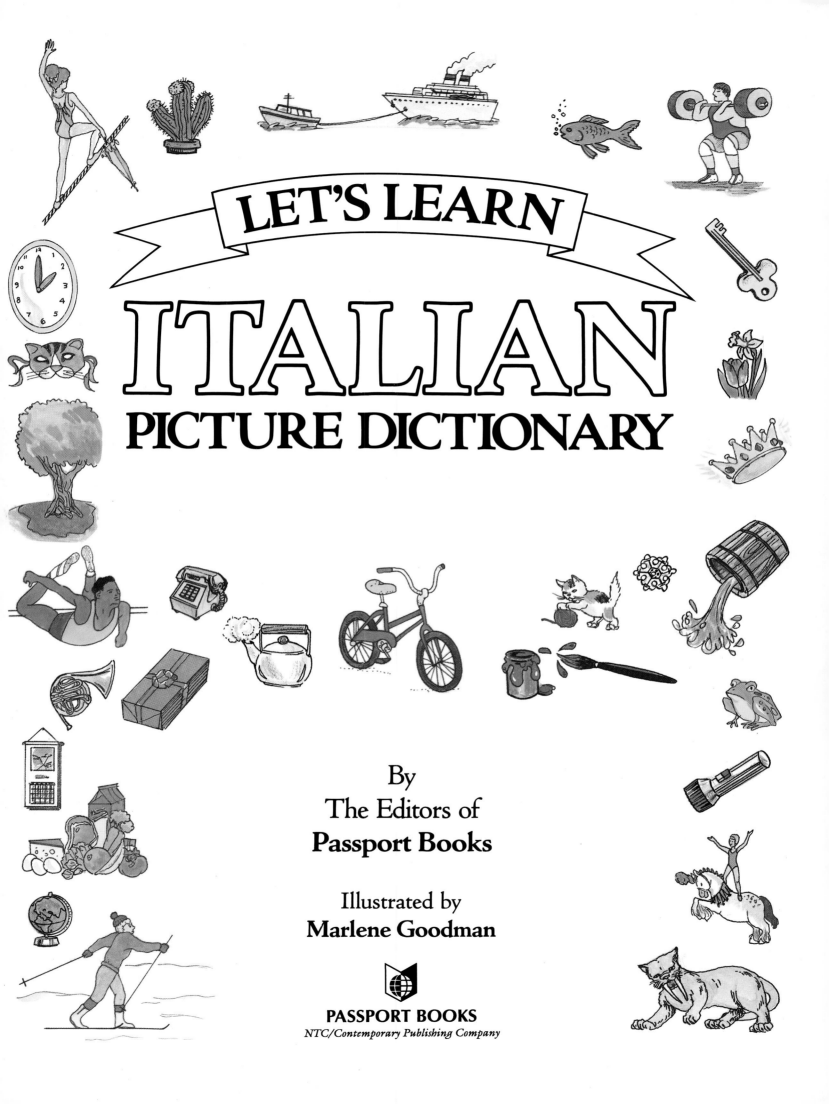

LET'S LEARN

ITALIAN
PICTURE DICTIONARY

By
The Editors of
Passport Books

Illustrated by
Marlene Goodman

PASSPORT BOOKS
NTC/Contemporary Publishing Company

Welcome to the *Let's Learn Italian* Picture Dictionary!

Here's an exciting way for you to learn more than 1,500 Italian words that will help you speak about many of your favorite subjects. With these words, you will be able to talk in Italian about your house, sports, outer space, the ocean, and many more subjects.

This dictionary is fun to use. On each page, you will see drawings with the Italian and English words that describe them underneath. These drawings are usually part of a large, colorful scene. See if you can find all the words in the big scene and then try to remember how to say each one in Italian. You will enjoy looking at the pictures more and more as you learn more Italian.

You will notice that almost all the Italian words in this book have **il, lo, l', gli, la,** or **le** before them. These words simply mean ''the''

and are usually used when you talk about things in Italian.

At the back of the book, you will find an Italian-English Glossary and Index and an English-Italian Glossary and Index, where you can look up words in alphabetical order, and find out exactly where the words are located in the dictionary. There is also a section that explains how you say Italian sounds as well as pronunciation guides that will help you say each Italian word correctly.

This is a book you can look at over and over again, and each time you look, you will find something new. You'll learn the Italian words for people, places, and things you know, and you may even learn some new words in English as you go along!

Library of Congress Cataloging-in-Publication Data
is available from the United States Library of Congress.

Illustrations by Terrie Meider
7. Clothing; 15. People in our Community; 18. Sports; 28. Colors;
29. The Family Tree; 30. Shapes; 31. Numbers; 32. Map of the World.

Published by Passport Books
An imprint of NTC/Contemporary Publishing Company
4255 West Touhy Avenue, Lincolnwood (Chicago), Illinois 60646-1975 U.S.A.
Copyright © 1991 by NTC/Contemporary Publishing Company
All rights reserved. No part of this book may be reproduced, stored in a retrieval
system, or transmitted in any form or by any means, electronic, mechanical,
photocopying, recording, or otherwise, without the prior permission of
NTC/Contemporary Publishing Company.
Printed in Hong Kong
International Standard Book Number: 0-8442-8065-8

8 9 0 WKT 12 11 10

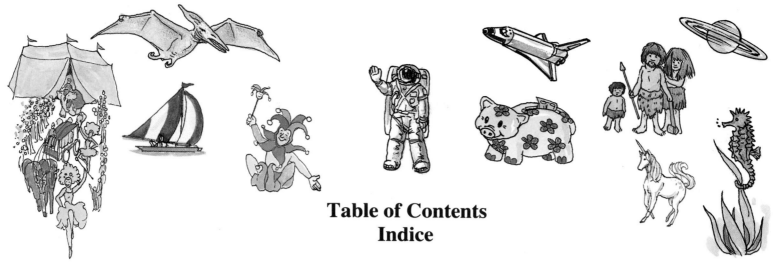

Table of Contents
Indice

1. Our Classroom Nostra Classe

teacher
il maestro
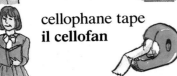

teacher
la maestra

student
l'alunno

student
l'alunna

map
la carta geografica

chalkboard
la lavagna

chalk
il gesso

(chalkboard) eraser
il cancellino
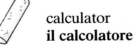

trash
la spazzatura

wastebasket
il cestino

stapler
l'aggraffatrice
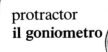

staples
le graffette
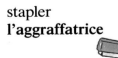

teacher's desk
la cattedra
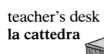

calendar
il calendario

cellophane tape
il cellofan

notebook
il quaderno

bookcase
lo scaffale

bulletin board
la bacheca

arithmetic problem
il problema d'aritmetica

calculator
il calcolatore

alphabet
l'alfabeto ABCD

easel
il cavalletto

protractor
il goniometro

pen
la penna

colored pencils
le matite colorate

pupil desk
il banco
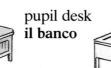

aquarium
l'acquario

fish
il pesce

loudspeaker
l'altoparlante

book
il libro

rug
il tappeto

ruler
la regola

scissors
le forbici

bell
la campanella

hole punch
la perforatrice per carta

compass
il compasso

(pencil) eraser
la gomma

pencil
la matita

pencil sharpener
il temperamatite
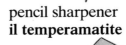

clock
l'orologio

hand
la lancetta
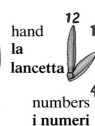

numbers
i numeri

cactu...
il cac...

plant
la pianta

glue
la colla

globe
il globo

picture
il quadro

paint
il colore

paintbrush
il pennello

paper
la carta

crayon
il pastello

2. Our House
La Nostra Casa

floor
il pavimento

wall
la parete

ceiling
il soffitto

door
la porta

shelf
lo scaffale

closet
**l'armadio
a muro**

hanger
l'attaccapanni

window
la finestra

stairs
le scale

medicine
cabinet
**l'armadietto
farmaceutico**

bathtub
la vasca

shower
la doccia

towel
l'asciugamano

toilet
la toletta

toilet paper
**la carta
igienica**

bed
il letto

blanket
**la coperta
di lana**

sheet
il lenzuolo

pillow
il guanciale

mirror
lo specchio

vase
il vaso

night table
il tavolo

alarm clock
la sveglia

rocking chair
**la sedia
a dondolo**

curtains
le tendine

venetian
blinds
le persiane

poster
il cartellone

chimney
il camino

roof
il tetto

armchair
la poltrona

sofa
il divano

television
il televisore

radio
la radio

fireplace
il focolare

carpet
il tappeto

footstool
il posapiedi

telephone
il telefono

lamp
la lampada

dresser
la toletta

record
il disco

compact disc
**il compact
disc**

record player
il giradischi

videocassette player
il videoregistratore

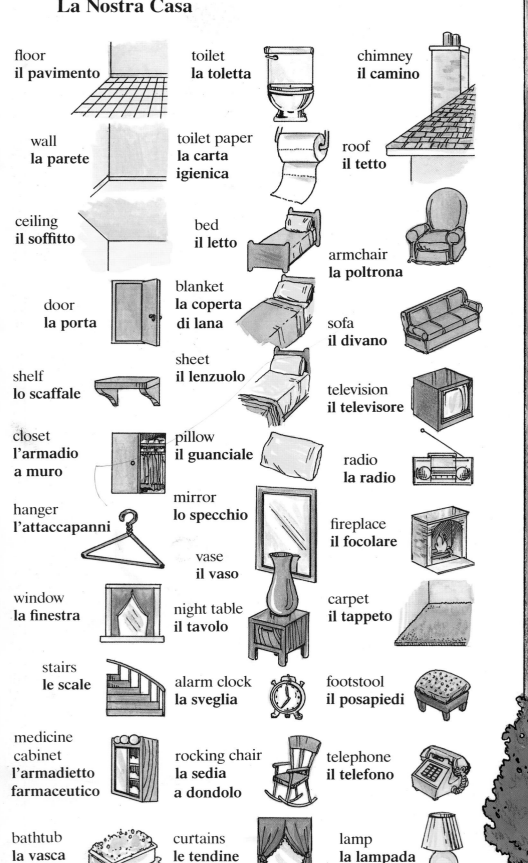

bedroom
la camera da letto

bathroom
la stanza da bagno

living room
il salotto

dining room
la sala da pranzo

kitchen
la cucina

cassette tape
la cassetta

cassette player
il magnetofono

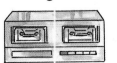
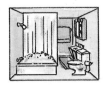

3. The Kitchen
La Cucina

counter
il banco

oven
il forno

faucet
il rubinetto

pan
la padella

paper towels
l'asciugamani di carta

chair
la sedia

table
la tavola

refrigerator
il frigorifero

dishwasher
il lavapiatti

electric mixer
il miscelatore

ice cubes
i ghiacci

apron
il grembiale

microwave oven
il forno a microonda

freezer
il congelatore

food processor
il food processor

drawer
il cassettino

spatula
la spatola

flour
la farina

stove
il fornello

sink
l'acquaio

kettle
il bollitore

toaster
il tostatore

dishes
i piatti

sponge
la spugna

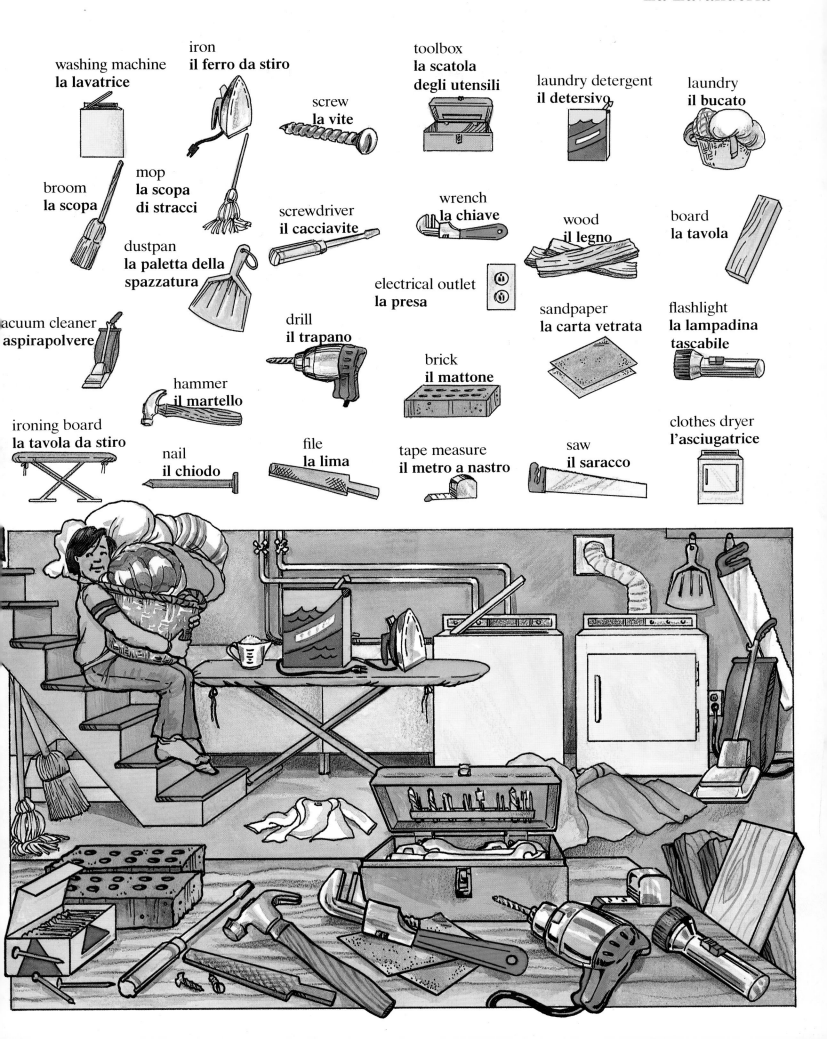

washing machine
la lavatrice

iron
il ferro da stiro

screw
la vite

toolbox
**la scatola
degli utensili**

laundry detergent
il detersivo

laundry
il bucato

broom
la scopa

mop
**la scopa
di stracci**

screwdriver
il cacciavite

wrench
la chiave

wood
il legno

board
la tavola

dustpan
**la paletta della
spazzatura**

electrical outlet
la presa

sandpaper
la carta vetrata

flashlight
**la lampadina
tascabile**

acuum cleaner
aspirapolvere

drill
il trapano

brick
il mattone

hammer
il martello

ironing board
la tavola da stiro

nail
il chiodo

file
la lima

tape measure
il metro a nastro

saw
il saracco

clothes dryer
l'asciugatrice

4. The Attic
La Soffitta

trunk **il baule**

game **il gioco**

coloring book **il libro di disegni**

box **la scatola**

doll **la bambola**

music box **la scatola della musica**

dust **il polvere**

jigsaw puzzle **il rompicapo**

yarn **la filaccia**

string **lo spago**

jump rope **la corda**

knitting needles **i ferri da calza**

cobweb **la ragnatela**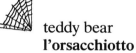

teddy bear **l'orsacchiotto**

dollhouse **la casa da bambole**

ball gown **il veste da ballo**

toys **i giocattoli**

comic books **i giornali a fumetti**

top hat **il cappello a cilindro**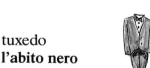

whistle **lo zufolo**

lightbulb **la lampadina**

tuxedo **l'abito nero**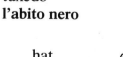

cards **le carte**

toy soldiers **i piccoli soldati**

hat **il cappello**

dice **i dadi**

movie projector **il proiettore**

feather **la piuma**

cowboy hat **il cappello di cowboy**

blocks **i blocchi**

umbrella **l'ombrello**

uniform **la divisa**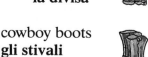

electric train **il trenino**

puppet **il burrattino**

cowboy boots **gli stivali di cowboy**

magnet **il magnete**

fan **il ventaglio**

rocking horse **il cavallo a dondolo**

chess **il gioco degli scacchi**

photo album **l'album di fotografie**

cradle **la culla**

marbles **le palline di marmo**

photograph
la foto

spinning wheel
il filatoio

picture frame
la cornice

rocking chair
la sedia a dondolo

checkers
il gioco della dama

5. The Four Seasons (Weather)
Le Quattro Stagioni (Il Tempo)

Winter
L'Inverno

snow **la neve**	sled **la slitta**
ice **il ghiaccio**	snowplow **lo spazzaneve**
snowflake **il fiocco di neve**	snowmobile **il gatto delle nevi**
icicle **il ghiacciolo**	snowman **l'uomo di neve**
shovel **la pala**	snowball **la palotta di neve**
snowstorm **il turbine di neve**	log **il ceppo**

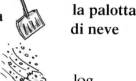

Spring
La Primavera

rain **la pioggia**	flowers **i fiori**
rainbow **l'arcobaleno**	
	flowerbed **l'aiuola**
stem **lo stelo**	petal **il petalo**
bird **l'uccello**	
worm **il verme**	vegetable garden **l'orto**
raindrop **la goccia di pioggia**	lightning **il fulmine**

Summer
l'Estate

butterfly
la farfalla

lawn mower
la falciatrice meccanica

fly
la mosca

barbecue
la griglia

fly swatter
il chiappamosche

hammock
l'amaca

fan
il ventilatore

yard
il cortile

sprinkler
lo spruzzatore

deck
la veranda

grasshopper
la cavalletta

garden hose
l'idrante

matches
i fiammiferi

Fall
L'Autunno

wind
il vento

kite
l'aquilone

leaf
la foglia

puddle
la pozzanghera

branch
il ramo

mud
il fango

fog
la nebbia

bird's nest
il nido

rake
il rastrello

clouds
le nuvole

bush
il cespuglio

6. At the Supermarket   Al Supermercato

vegetables
gli ortaggi

fruit
le frutta

meat
la carne

cabbage
il cavolo

apple
la mela

eggs
le uova

lettuce
la lattuga

orange
l'arancia

butter
il burro

green beans
i fagiolini

lemon
il limone

bread
il pane

peas
i piselli

lime
il tiglio

cheese
il formaggio

carrots
le carote

cherries
le ciliege

food
il cibo

tomatoes
i pomodori

banana
la banana

potatoes
le patate

grapes
le uva

milk
il latte

onions
le cipolle

strawberries
le fragole

cookies
i biscotti

spinach
gli spinaci

peach
la pesca

crackers
i crackers

avocado
l'avocado

grapefruit
il pompelmo

potato chips
le patatine

nuts
le noci

melon
il melone

bottle
la bottiglia

chocolate
la cioccolata

watermelon
il cocomero

fruit juice
il succo

candy
le caramelle

raspberries
i lamponi

cereal
i cereali

frozen dinner
il pranzo surgelato

soap
il sapone

money
il denaro

pie
la torta

pineapple
l'ananas

can
la scatola

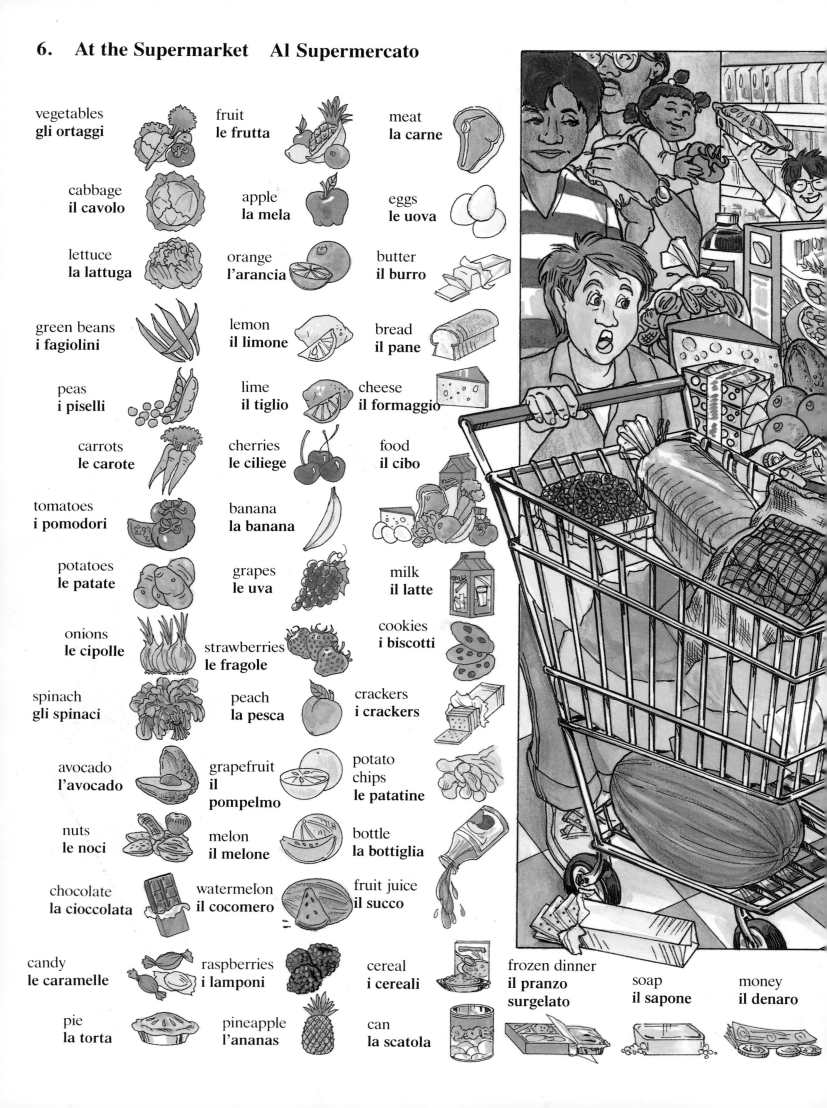

shopping cart
il carrello

shopping
bag
**il pacco
per la spesa**

sign
il cartellino

scale
la bilancia

price
il prezzo

cash register
la cassa

cashier
la cassiere

7. Clothing   Abiti

glasses
gli occhiali

buckle
la fibbia

belt
la cintura

collar
il collo

blouse
la camicetta

bracelet
il braccialetto

ring
l'anello

skirt
la gonna

pants
i pantaloni

socks
i calzini

shoes
le scarpe

underwear
la biancheria intima

tie
la cravatta

necklace
la collana

sleeve
la manica

dress
il vestito

suit
il completo

bathing suit
il costume da bagno

button
il bottone

shirt
la camicia

earmuffs
il paraorecchie

gloves
i guanti

handkerchief
il fazzoletto

shoelace
la stringa

coat
il cappotto

sweater
il golf

gym shoes
le scarpe da tennis

tights
la calzamaglia

hat
il cappello

sunglasses
gli occhiali scuri

earring
l'orecchino

sweatshirt
la maglietta sportiva

hood
il cappuccio

raincoat
l'impermeabile

shorts
i calzoncini corti

pocket
la tasca

zipper
la cerniera

sweatpants
i pantaloni della tuta

sandals
i sandali

T-shirt
la maglietta

boots
gli stivali

backpack
lo zaino

umbrella
l'ombrello

watch
l'orologio

down vest
il gilè di piuma

scarf
la sciarpa

bathrobe
l'accappatoio

pajamas
la pigiama

jeans
i jeans

jacket
la giacca

mittens
i guanti a manopola

hiking boots
gli scarponi

cap
il cappello da sci

8. In the City   Nella Città

building
l'edificio

apartment building
l'edificio degli appartamenti

train station
la stazione

skyscraper
il grattacielo

fire escape
la scala di sicurezza

church
la chiesa

factory
la fabbrica

balcony
il balcone

school
la scuola

smokestack
il fumaiolo

fire station
la stazione dei pompieri

museum
il museo

traffic lights
il semaforo

police station
il posto di polizia

hospital
l'ospedale

manhole cover
la bocca di accesso

jail
il carcere

drugstore (pharmacy)
la farmacia

bookstore
la libreria

driveway
la strada privata

toy store
il negozio dei gioccattoli

movie theater
il cinema

parking lot
il parcheggio

grocery store
la drogheria

restaurant
il ristorante

parking meter
il parchimetro

clothing store
il negozio di confezioni

corner
l'angolo

bakery
la panetteria

fire hydrant
l'idrante

butcher shop
la macelleria

hotel
l'albergo

square
la piazza

fountain
la fontana

traffic jam
l'intasamento

statue
la statua

newspaper
il giornale

crane
la gru

bench
la panca

sign
il segnale

playground
il parco giochi

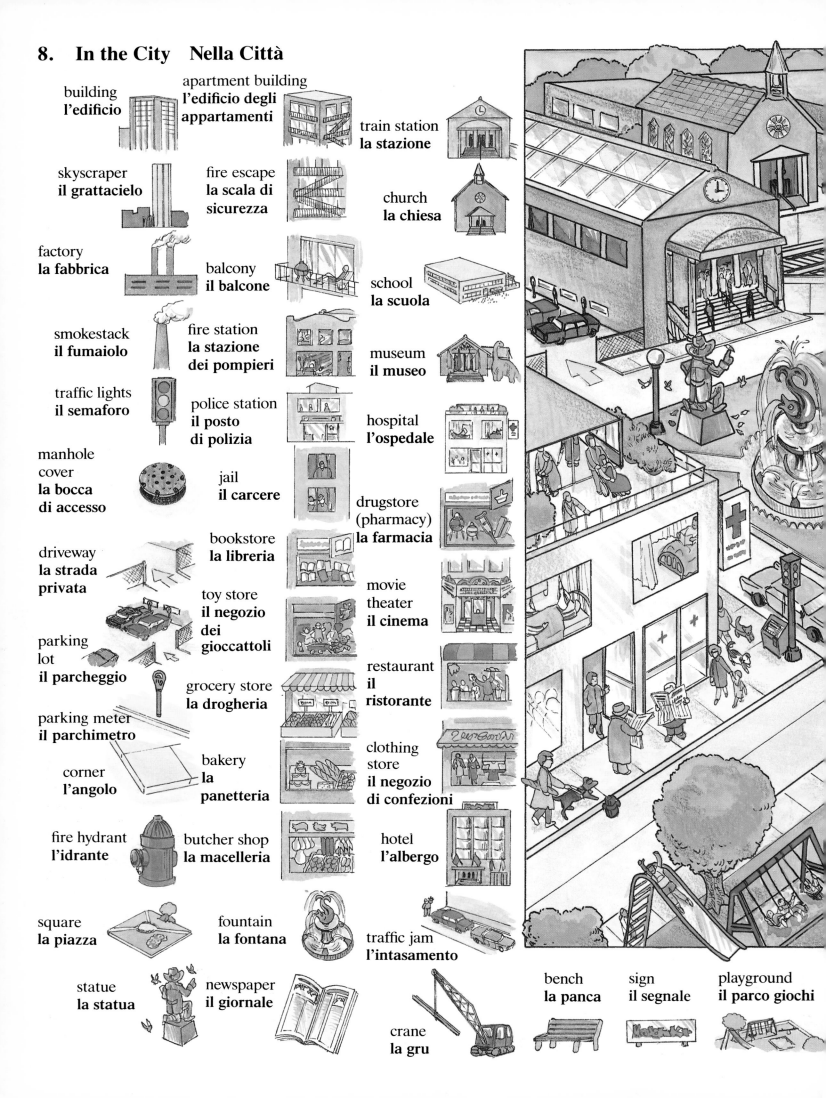

park	jungle gym	swings	seesaw	slide	sandbox	beach
il parco	**l'attrezzo ginnico**	**l'altalena**	**il su in giù**	**la scivola**	**il recinto con sabbia**	**la spiaggia**

9. In the Country   In Paese

farmer
l'agricoltore

tractor
il trattore

barn
il granaio

hay
il fieno

dog
il cane

puppy
il cucciolo

cat
il gatto

kitten
il gattino

rooster
il gallo

hen
la gallina

chick
il pulcino

pig
il maiale

piglet
il porcellino

rabbit
il coniglio

bull
il toro

cow
la mucca

calf
il vitello

horse
il cavallo

colt
il puledro

duck
l'anitra

duckling
l'anatroccolo

goat
la capra

kid
il capretto

goose
l'oca

gosling
il papero

sheep
la pecora

lamb
l'agnello

mouse
il topo

horns
le corna

donkey
l'asino

bees
le api

frog
la rana

pond
lo stagno

grass
l'erba

fence
il recinto

tree
l'albero

shadow
l'ombra

hill
la collina

road
la strada

smoke
il fumo

picnic
il picnic

ant
la formica

dirt
la terra

tent
la tenda

sky
il cielo

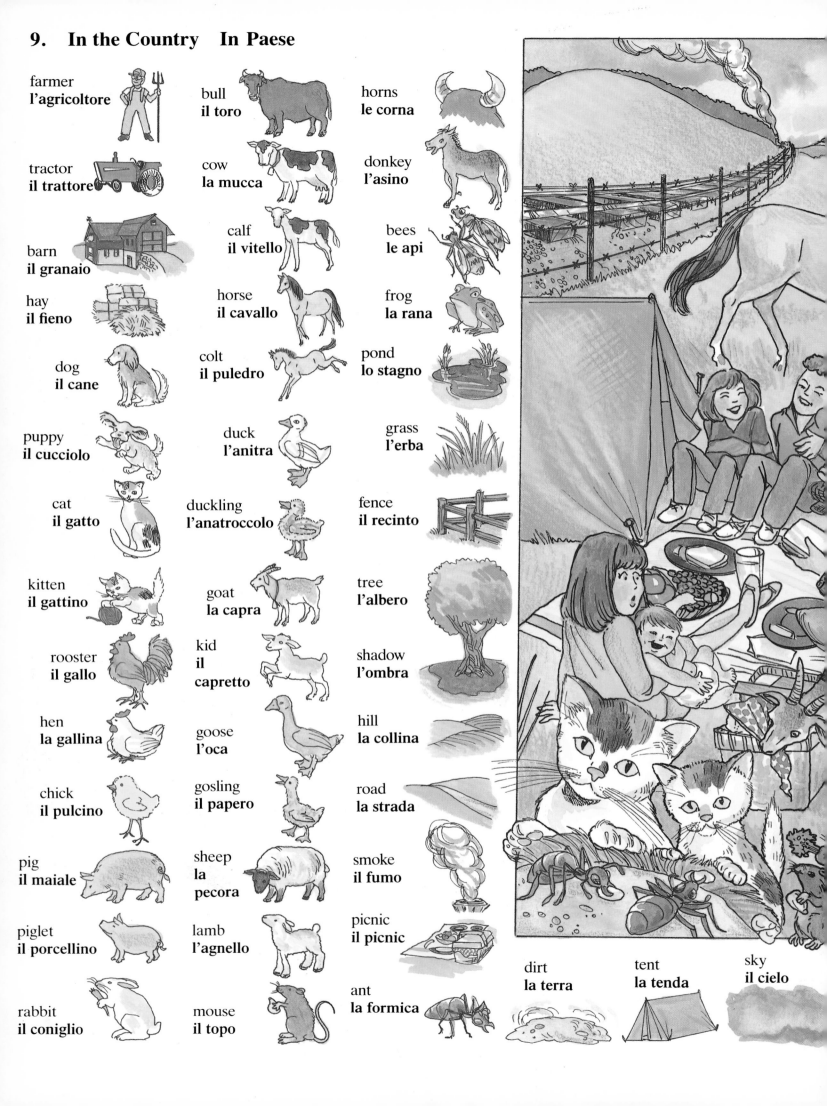

train tracks
le rotaie

sleeping bag
il sacco a pelo

boy
il ragazzo

man
l'uomo

woman
la donna

girl
la ragazza

baby
il piccino

farm
la fattoria

10. In a Restaurant   Al Ristorante

breakfast **la colazione**

lunch **il pranzo**

dinner **la cena**

yolk **il rosso d'uovo**

hamburger **la svizzera**

steak **la bistecca**

omelet **la frittata**

sandwich **il tramezzino**

fish **il pesce**

toast **il crostino**

french fries **le patatine fritte**

ham **il prosciutto**

jam **la marmellata**

soup **la zuppa**

chicken **il pollo**

sausages **le salsiccie**

noodles **la pasta**

broccoli **i broccoletti**

coffee **il caffè**

ketchup **il ketchup**

celery **il sedano**

tea **il tè**

mustard **la mostarda**

salad **l'insalata**

cream **la panna**

salt **il sale**

rice **il riso**

sugar **lo zucchero**

pepper **il pepe**

mushroom **il fungo**

meals **i pasti**

ice cream **il gelato**

tray **il vassoio**

waiter **il cameriere**

candle **la candela**

tablecloth **la tovaglia**

waitress **la cameriera**

cake **la torta**

straw **la cannuccia**

gift **il regalo**

birthday party **la festa di compleanno**

soft drink **la bevanda**

knife **il coltello**

fork **la forchetta**

spoon **il cucchiaio**

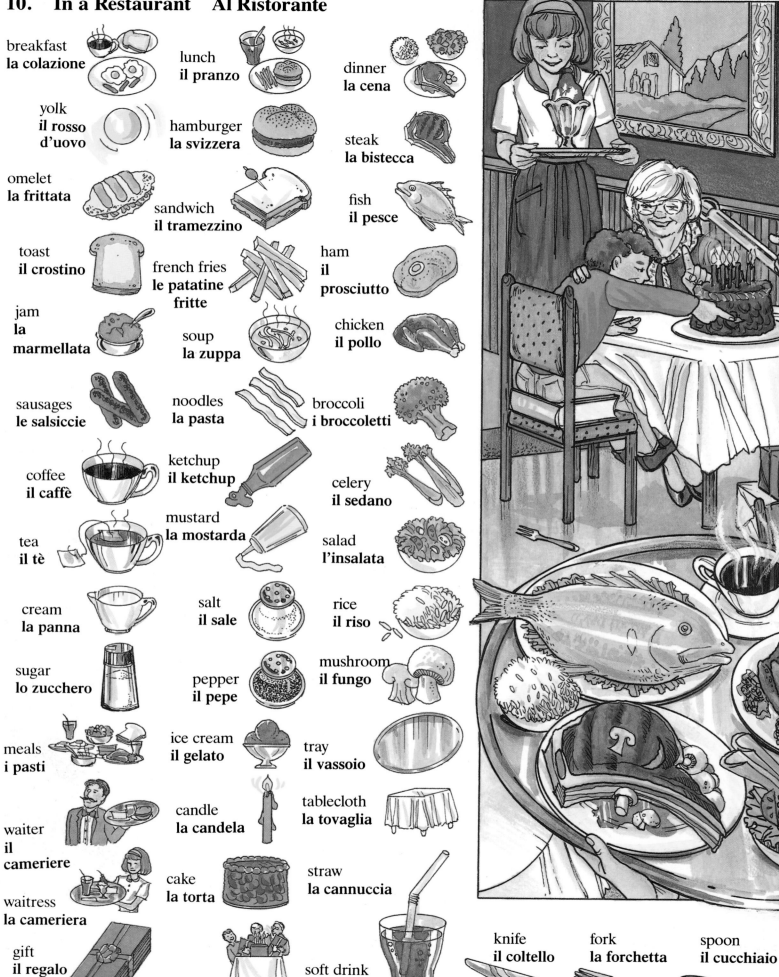

plate
il piatto

saucer
il piattino

cup
la tazza

glass
il bicchiere

bowl
la scodella

napkin
il tovagliolo

menu
il menù

11. The Doctor's Office   Dal Medico

doctor
la dottoressa

nurse
l'infermiere

patient
il paziente

medicine
la medicina

pill
la pillola

thermometer
il termometro

bandage
**il cerotto
medicato**

cast
il gesso

sling
**il bendaggio
a fionda**

hypodermic needle
l'ago

blood
il sangue

cane
il bastone

crutch
la gruccia

stethoscope
lo stetoscopio

examining
table
**la tavola da
esaminare**

sneeze
lo starnuto

arm
il braccio

elbow
il gomito

hand
la mano

finger
il dito

thumb
il pollice

leg
la gamba

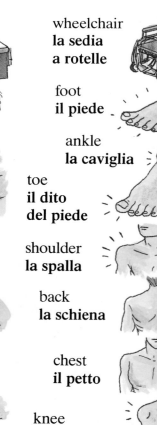

wheelchair
**la sedia
a rotelle**

foot
il piede

ankle
la caviglia

toe
**il dito
del piede**

shoulder
la spalla

back
la schiena

chest
il petto

knee
il ginocchio

The Dentist's Office   Dal Dentista

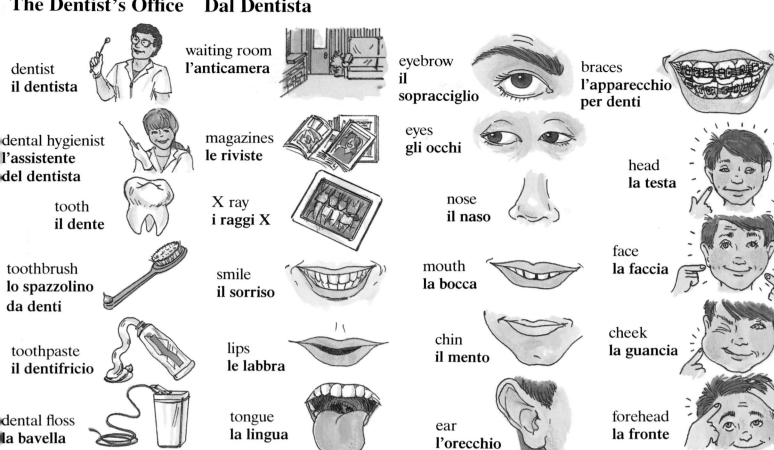

dentist
il dentista

waiting room
l'anticamera

eyebrow
il sopracciglio

braces
l'apparecchio per denti

dental hygienist
l'assistente del dentista

magazines
le riviste

eyes
gli occhi

tooth
il dente

X ray
i raggi X

nose
il naso

head
la testa

toothbrush
lo spazzolino da denti

smile
il sorriso

mouth
la bocca

face
la faccia

toothpaste
il dentifricio

lips
le labbra

chin
il mento

cheek
la guancia

dental floss
la bavella

tongue
la lingua

ear
l'orecchio

forehead
la fronte

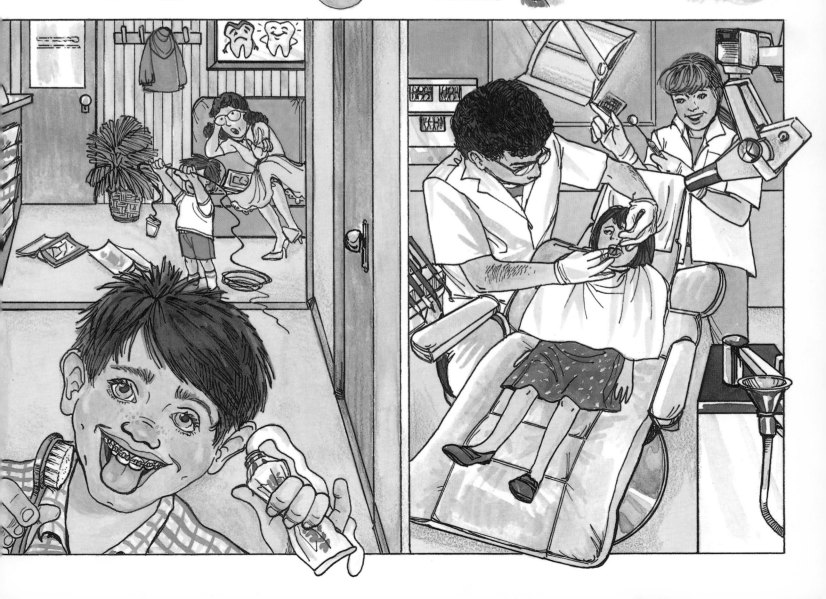

12. The Barber Shop/Beauty Salon
Dal Barbiere/Istituto di Bellezza

hairstylist
la parrucchiera

shampoo
lo shampoo

suds
la schiuma di sapone

comb
il pettine

brush
la spazzola

scissors
le forbici

curlers
i bigodini

curling iron
il ferro per arricciare i capelli

barber
il barbiere

shaving cream
la crema da barba

razor
il rasoio

beard
la barba

mousse
il mousse

manicurist
la manicure

fingernail
l'unghia

nail polish
lo smalto

lipstick
il rossetto

mascara
la mascara

powder
la cipra

hair dryer
l'asciugacapelli

bald
calvo

mustache
i baffi

freckles
le lentiggini

pedicurist
la pedicure

barrette
il fermacapelli

braid
la treccia

wavy
ondulati

straight
lisci

curly
ricci

short
corti

long
lunghi

black
neri

brown
castagni

blond
biondi

red
rossi

toenail
l'unghia del piede

nail clippers
il tagliaunghie

nail file
la limaiola

crew cut
il taglio a spazzola

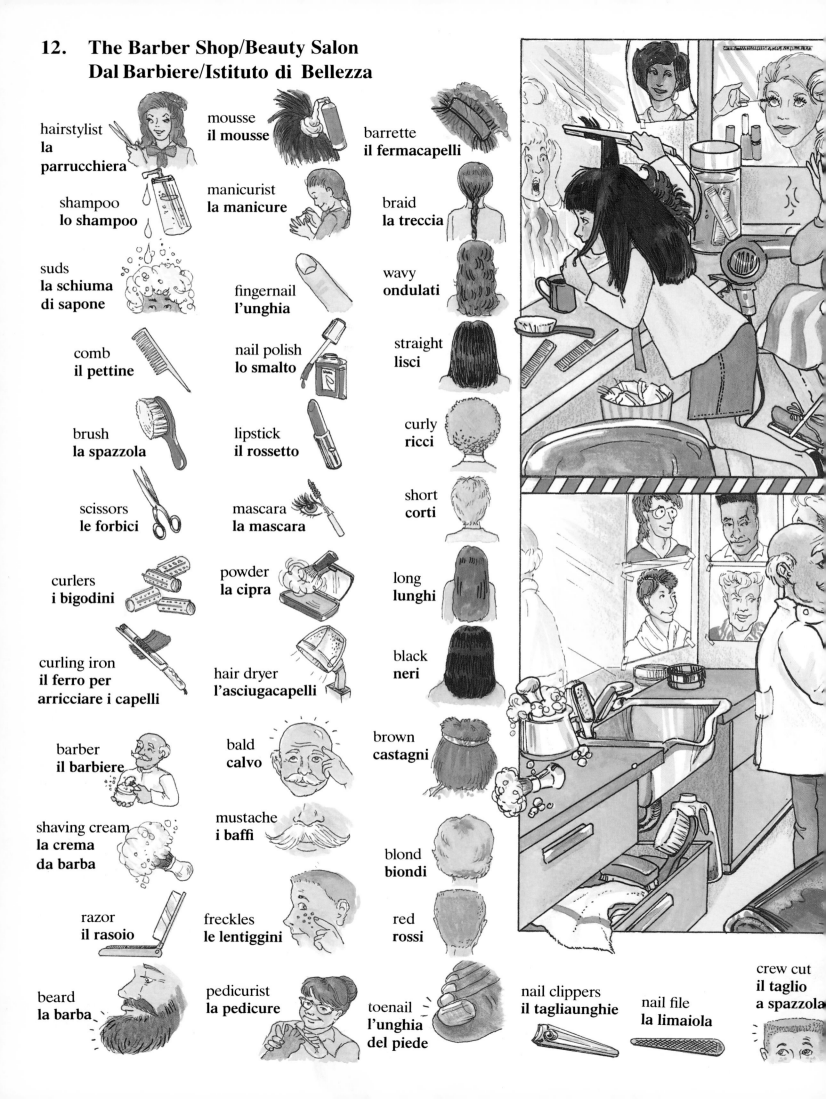

ponytail
**la coda
di cavallo**

bangs
la frangia

bun
il chignon

part
la scriminatura

hair spray
lo spruzzo

hair
i capelli

blow dryer
il fon

13. The Post Office L'Ufficio Postale

packing tape
il nastro d'imballaggio

package
il pacco

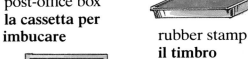

scale
la bilancia

ink pad
il tampone

post-office box
la cassetta per imbucare

rubber stamp
il timbro

label
l'etichetta

rubber band
l'elastico

letter
la lettera

postcard
la cartolina

string
lo spago

knot
il nodo

bow
il fiocco

postmark
il timbro postale

phone booth
la cabina telefonica

return address
l'indirizzo del mittente

address
l'indirizzo

mailbox
la cassetta postale

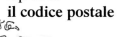

zip code
il codice postale

mail slot
il buco delle lettere

60016

mailbag
il sacco da posta

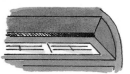

postal worker
l'impiegato dell'ufficio postale

stamp
il francobollo

The Bank   La Banca

paper clip
la graffa

security guard
la guardia

security camera
la telecamera di sicurezza

safe
la cassaforte

credit card
la carta di credito

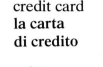

typewriter
la macchina da scrivere

safety deposit box
la cassetta di sicurezza

notepad
il blocco

teller
il cassiere

wallet
il portafoglio
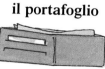

key
la chiave

lock
la serratura

file cabinet
lo schedario

receptionist
la segretaria

bill
il biglietto

coin
la moneta

check
l'assegno

checkbook
il libretto d'assegni

piggy bank
il salvadanaio

signature
la firma

drive-in
il servizio per le automobili

automatic teller
il bancomat

14. At the Gas Station   Alla Stazione di Servizio

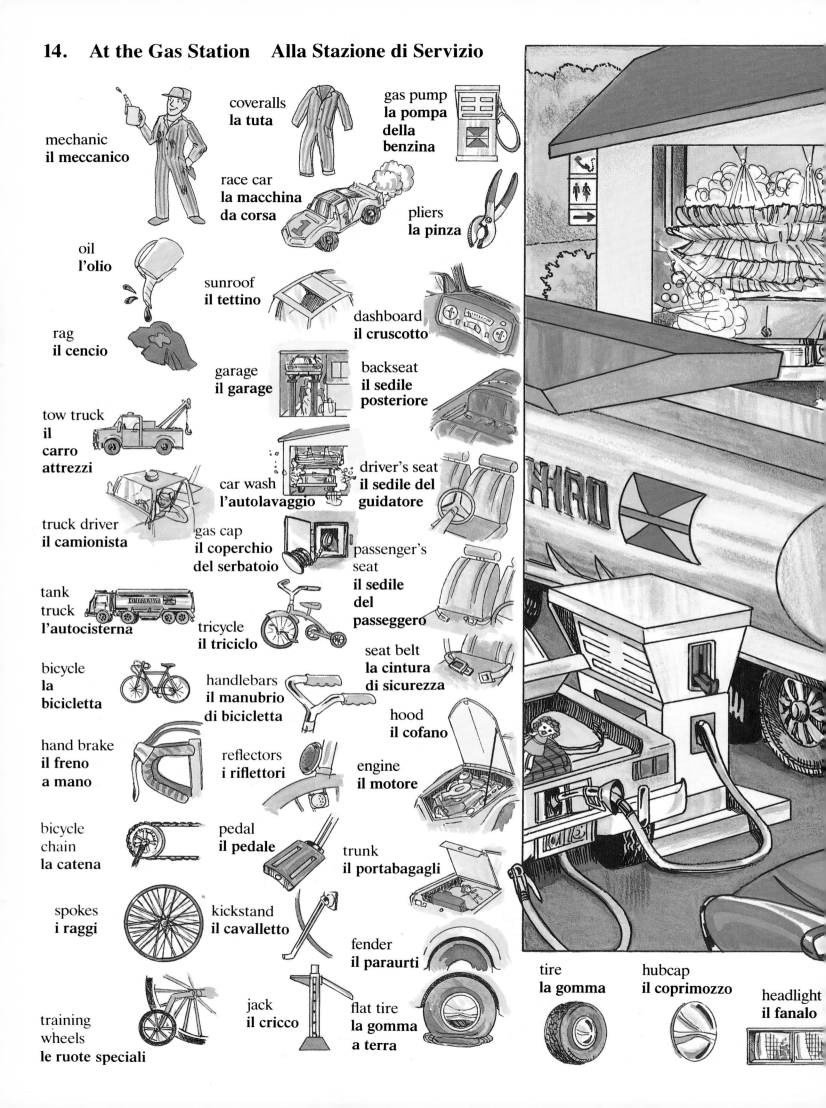

mechanic
il meccanico

coveralls
la tuta

gas pump
la pompa della benzina

race car
la macchina da corsa

pliers
la pinza

oil
l'olio

rag
il cencio

sunroof
il tettino

dashboard
il cruscotto

garage
il garage

backseat
il sedile posteriore

tow truck
il carro attrezzi

car wash
l'autolavaggio

driver's seat
il sedile del guidatore

truck driver
il camionista

gas cap
il coperchio del serbatoio

passenger's seat
il sedile del passeggero

tank truck
l'autocisterna

tricycle
il triciclo

seat belt
la cintura di sicurezza

bicycle
la bicicletta

handlebars
il manubrio di bicicletta

hood
il cofano

hand brake
il freno a mano

reflectors
i riflettori

engine
il motore

bicycle chain
la catena

pedal
il pedale

trunk
il portabagagli

spokes
i raggi

kickstand
il cavalletto

fender
il paraurti

training wheels
le ruote speciali

jack
il cricco

flat tire
la gomma a terra

tire
la gomma

hubcap
il coprimozzo

headlight
il fanalo

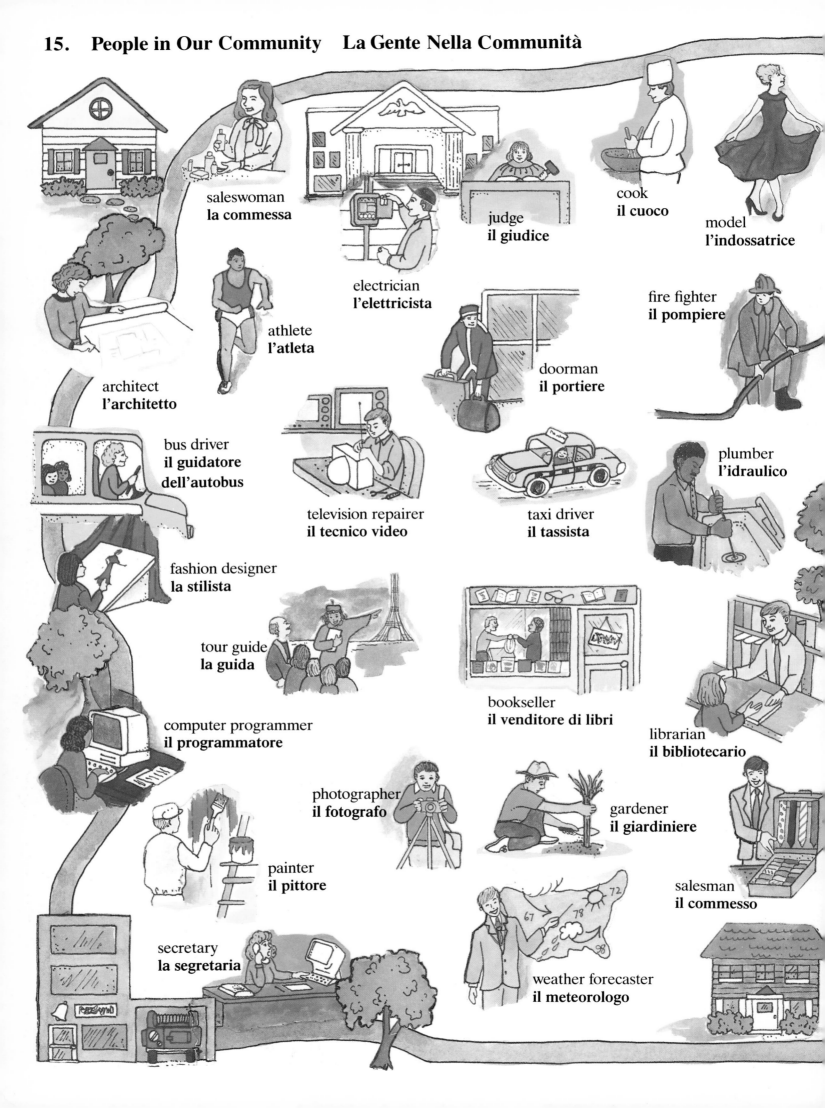

saleswoman
la commessa

judge
il giudice

cook
il cuoco

model
l'indossatrice

electrician
l'elettricista

athlete
l'atleta

doorman
il portiere

fire fighter
il pompiere

architect
l'architetto

bus driver
il guidatore dell'autobus

television repairer
il tecnico video

taxi driver
il tassista

plumber
l'idraulico

fashion designer
la stilista

tour guide
la guida

bookseller
il venditore di libri

librarian
il bibliotecario

computer programmer
il programmatore

photographer
il fotografo

gardener
il giardiniere

painter
il pittore

salesman
il commesso

secretary
la segretaria

weather forecaster
il meteorologo

policewoman
**la donna
poliziotto**

veterinarian
il veterinario

disc jockey
il disc jockey

reporter
il cronista

construction worker
il manovale

florist
la fiorista

tailor
il sarto

factory worker
l'operaia

butcher
il macellaio

optician
l'ottico

jeweler
il gioielliere

foreman
il capomastro

carpenter
il falegname

banker
il banchiere

artist
l'artista

pharmacist
la farmacista

sailor
il marinaio

lawyer
l'avvocatessa

paramedic
**l'assistente
del medico**

letter carrier
il postino

fisherman
il pescatore

cowboy
il cowboy

policeman
il poliziotto

astronomer
l'astronomo

16. Going Places (Transportation) Trasporto

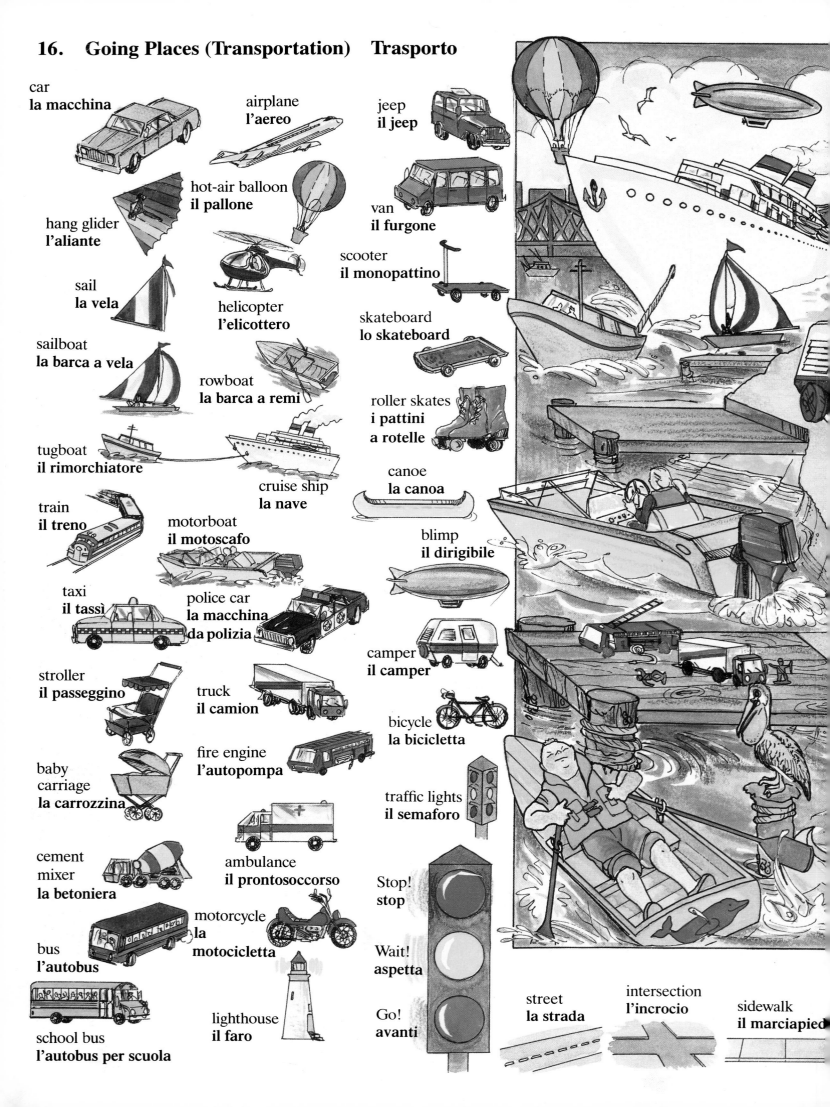

car
la macchina

airplane
l'aereo

jeep
il jeep

hot-air balloon
il pallone

van
il furgone

hang glider
l'aliante

scooter
il monopattino

sail
la vela

helicopter
l'elicottero

skateboard
lo skateboard

sailboat
la barca a vela

rowboat
la barca a remi

roller skates
**i pattini
a rotelle**

tugboat
il rimorchiatore

canoe
la canoa

cruise ship
la nave

train
il treno

motorboat
il motoscafo

blimp
il dirigibile

taxi
il tassì

police car
**la macchina
da polizia**

camper
il camper

stroller
il passeggino

truck
il camion

bicycle
la bicicletta

baby
carriage
la carrozzina

fire engine
l'autopompa

traffic lights
il semaforo

cement
mixer
la betoniera

ambulance
il prontosoccorso

Stop!
stop

bus
l'autobus

motorcycle
**la
motocicletta**

Wait!
aspetta

school bus
l'autobus per scuola

lighthouse
il faro

Go!
avanti

street
la strada

intersection
l'incrocio

sidewalk
il marciapied

dock
il molo

bus stop
la fermata

bridge
il ponte

crosswalk
il passaggio pedonale

oar
il remo

boat
la barca

stop sign
lo stop

17. The Airport   L'Aeroporto

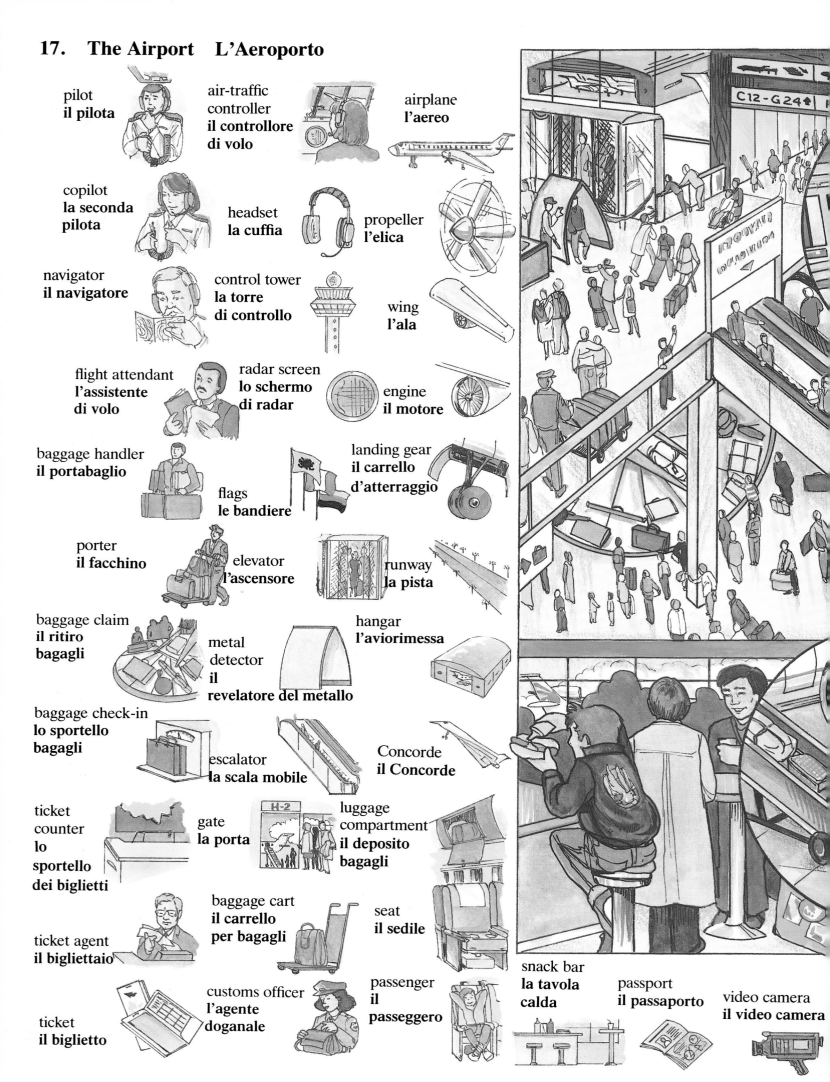

pilot
il pilota

air-traffic controller
il controllore di volo

airplane
l'aereo

copilot
la seconda pilota

headset
la cuffia

propeller
l'elica

navigator
il navigatore

control tower
la torre di controllo

wing
l'ala

flight attendant
l'assistente di volo

radar screen
lo schermo di radar

engine
il motore

baggage handler
il portabaglio

flags
le bandiere

landing gear
il carrello d'atterraggio

porter
il facchino

elevator
l'ascensore

runway
la pista

baggage claim
il ritiro bagagli

metal detector
il revelatore del metallo

hangar
l'aviorimessa

baggage check-in
lo sportello bagagli

escalator
la scala mobile

Concorde
il Concorde

ticket counter
lo sportello dei biglietti

gate
la porta

luggage compartment
il deposito bagagli

seat
il sedile

ticket agent
il bigliettaio

baggage cart
il carrello per bagagli

ticket
il biglietto

customs officer
l'agente doganale

passenger
il passeggero

snack bar
la tavola calda

passport
il passaporto

video camera
il video camera

tennis racket
la racchetta

binoculars
il binocolo

camera
la macchina fotografica

purse
la borsa

suitcase
la valigia

garment bag
il sacco per abiti

briefcase
la borsa per documenti

18. Sports Sport

gymnastics
la ginnastica

goggles
gli occhiali di protezione

wrestling
la lotta sportiva

cross-country skiing
il fondo

cycling
il ciclismo

soccer
il calcio

long jump
il salto in lungo

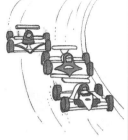
car racing
la corsa

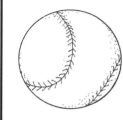
baseball
la palla

boxing
il pugilato

badminton
il volano

net
la rete

football
il football americano

skates
i pattini

skating
il pattinaggio

hurdles
la corsa a ostacoli

golf
il golf

medal
la medaglia

horseback riding
l'equitazione

baseball
il baseball

jogging
il footing

hockey
l' hockey

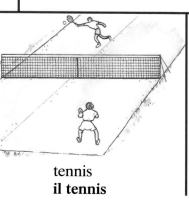
tennis
il tennis

diving
il tuffarsi

weight lifting
il sollevamento di pesi

umpire
l'arbitro

bowling
il gioco dei birilli automatici

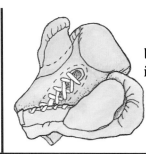

boxing gloves
i guantoni

high jump
il salto in alto

table tennis
il ping-pong

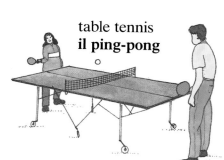

skydiving
il paracadutismo

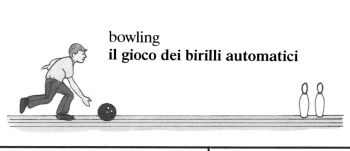

soccer ball
la palla

bat
la mazza

football
la palla

parachute
il paracadute

swimming pool
la piscina

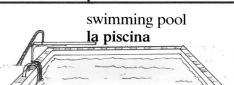

running
il correre

downhill skiing
lo sci alpino

golf club
la mazza da golf

trophy
il trofeo

horse racing
la corsa da cavalli

helmet
l'elmetto

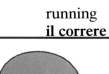

bicycle
la bicicletta

skis
gli sci

sailing
l'andare a vela

basketball
la pallacanestro

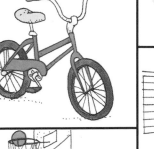

volleyball
la pallavolo

swimming
il nuoto

racket
la racchetta

referee
l'arbitro

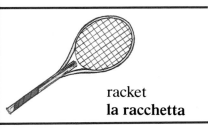

19. The Talent Show   La Mostra dei Talenti

actor
l'attore

actress
l'attrice

children
i ragazzi

auditorium
l'auditorio

audience
il pubblico

singer
il cantante

stage
il palcoscenico

curtain
il sipario

dancer
la ballerina

scenery
il scenario

script
il copione

ballet slippers
le scarpette da ballo

spotlight
il fascio di luce

dressing room
il camerino

tutu
il tutù

rope
la corda

sewing machine
la macchina per cucire

leotard
la calzamaglia

microphone
il microfono

master of ceremonies
il cerimoniere

costume
il costume

makeup
il trucco

orchestra pit
la buca dell' orchestra

mask
la maschera

sheet music
le carte di musica

orchestra
l'orchestra

wig
la parrucca

conductor
il direttore d'orchestra

accordion
la fisarmonica

cymbals
i piatti

French horn
il cornetto

trumpet
la tromba

saxophone
il sassofono

xylophone
il silofono

violin
il violino

bow
l'archetto

guitar
la chitarra

drum
il tamburo

piano
il pianoforte

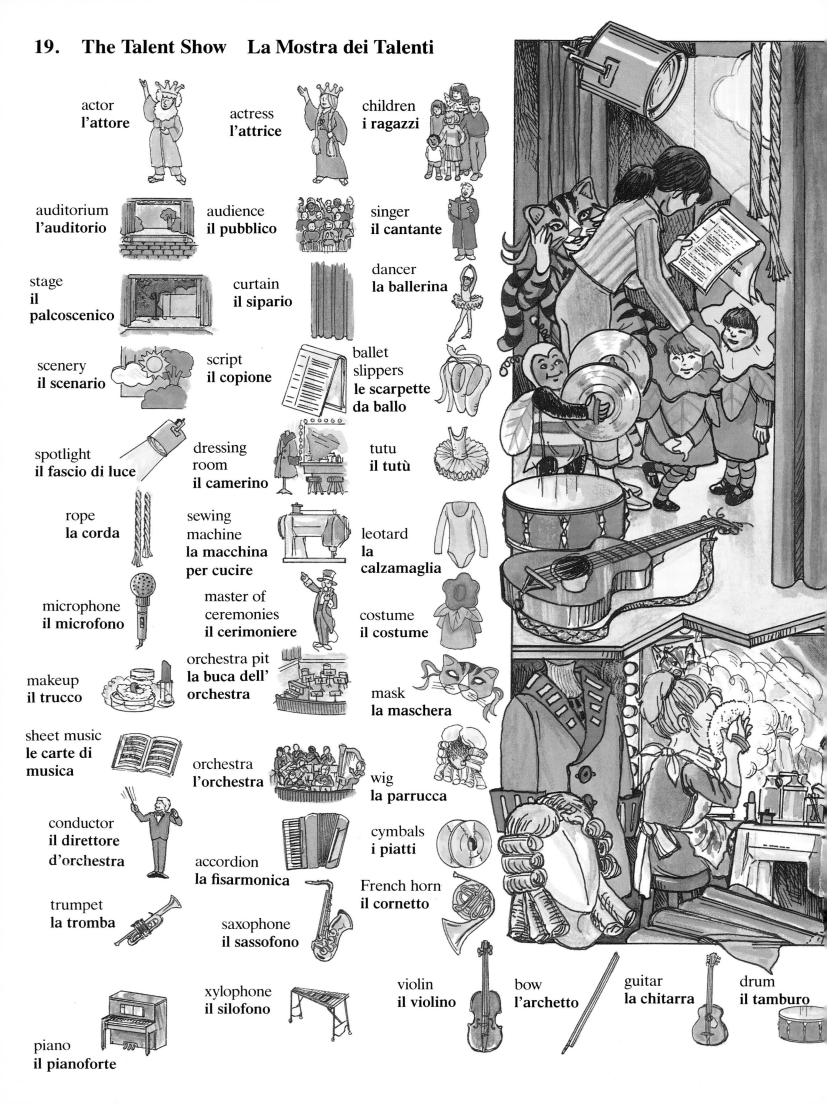

tuba
la tuba

flute
il flauto

trombone
il trombone

clarinet
il clarinetto

cello
il violoncello

strings
la corda

harp
l'arpa

20. At the Zoo   Allo Zoo

zookeeper
lo zoologo

elephant
l'elefante

animals
gli animali

rhinoceros
il rinoceronte

ostrich
lo struzzo

fox
la volpe

lion
il leone

bear
l'orso

wolf
il lupo

tiger
la tigre

bear cub
l'orsacchiotto

alligator
il coccodrillo

tiger cub
il tigrotto

polar bear
l'orso bianco

zebra
la zebra

jaguar
il giaguaro

panda
l'orso panda

giraffe
la giraffa

leopard
il gattopardo

gorilla
il gorilla

monkey
la scimmia

flamingo
il fenicottero

parrot
il pappagallo

hippopotamus
l'ippopotamo

owl
il gufo

snake
il serpente

kangaroo
il canguro

swan
il cigno

seal
la foca

deer
il cervo

penguin
il pinguino

walrus
il tricheco

lizard
la lucertola

peacock
il pavone

hump
la gobba

turtle
la tartaruga

eagle
l'aquila

camel
il cammello

horns
le corna

wings
le ali

feathers
le piume

beak
il becco

paw
la zampa

claws
l'artiglio

mane
la criniera

tail
la coda

hoof
lo zoccolo

stripes
le striscie

spots
le macchie

21. At the Circus   Al Circo

clown
il pagliaccio

popcorn
il popcorn

caramel apple
la mela caramellata

balloon
il pallone

peanuts
le arachidi

film
la pellicola

magician
il mago

lion
il leone

tent pole
l'asta della tenda

elephant
l'elefante

flashbulb
il riflettore

camera
la macchina fotografica

juggler
il giocoliere

tickets
i biglietti

baton
il battone

turban
il turbano

lightbulb
la lampadina

night
la notte

ticket booth
la biglietteria

stilts
i trampoli

big top
la tenda

circus parade
la parata di circo

rest rooms
i gabinetti

bareback rider
**la cavallerizza
senza sella**

tightrope walker
la funambola

tightrope
**la corda tesa
per funamboli**

handstand
la verticale

headstand
**la verticale
sulla testa**

trapeze
il trapezio

acrobat
l'acrobata

somersault
**il salto
mortale**

trapeze artist
il trapezista

cage
la gabbia

ring
l'arena

cartwheel
**la ruota di
carretta**

safety net
**la rete di
sicurezza**

hoop
il cerchio

cotton candy
**lo zucchero
filato**

band
la banda

rope ladder
**la scala per
arrampicarsi**

cape
la mantellina

whip
la frusta

lion tamer
**il domatore
dei leoni**

unicycle
l'uniciclo

rope
la corda

ringmaster
il presentatore

22. In the Ocean
L'Oceano

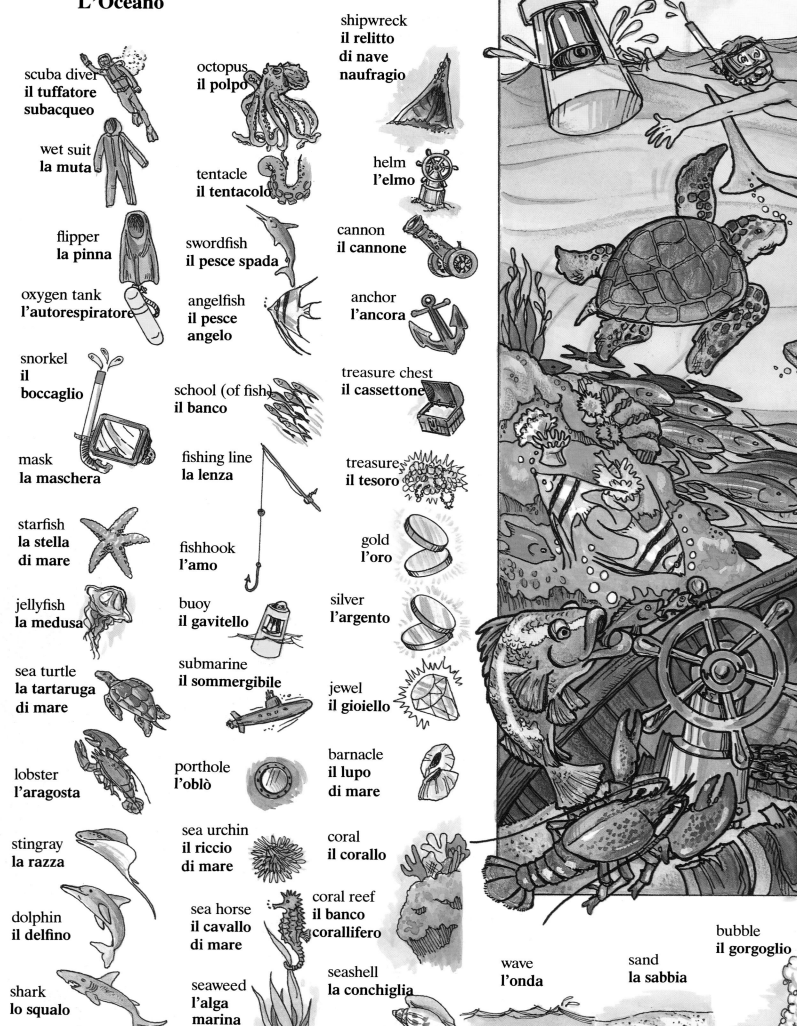

scuba diver
il tuffatore subacqueo

wet suit
la muta

flipper
la pinna

oxygen tank
l'autorespiratore

snorkel
il boccaglio

mask
la maschera

starfish
la stella di mare

jellyfish
la medusa

sea turtle
la tartaruga di mare

lobster
l'aragosta

stingray
la razza

dolphin
il delfino

shark
lo squalo

octopus
il polpo

tentacle
il tentacolo

swordfish
il pesce spada

angelfish
il pesce angelo

school (of fish)
il banco

fishing line
la lenza

fishhook
l'amo

buoy
il gavitello

submarine
il sommergibile

porthole
l'oblò

sea urchin
il riccio di mare

sea horse
il cavallo di mare

seaweed
l'alga marina

shipwreck
il relitto di nave naufragio

helm
l'elmo

cannon
il cannone

anchor
l'ancora

treasure chest
il cassettone

treasure
il tesoro

gold
l'oro

silver
l'argento

jewel
il gioiello

barnacle
il lupo di mare

coral
il corallo

coral reef
il banco corallifero

seashell
la conchiglia

wave
l'onda

sand
la sabbia

bubble
il gorgoglio

ales
scaglie

gills
le branchie

fin
la pinna

clam
l'ostrica

crab
il granchio

squid
il calamaro

whale
la balena

23. Space
Lo Spazio

astronaut
l'astronauta
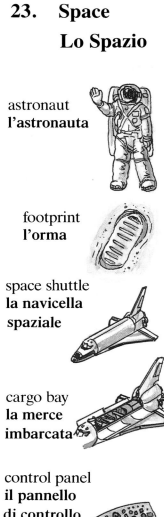

space suit
la tuta spaziale

space helmet
l'elmo spaziale

footprint
l'orma

space walk
il passeggio nello spazio

moon rock
il cristallo di luna

space shuttle
la navicella spaziale

lunar rover
la macchina lunare

laboratory
il laboratorio

cargo bay
la merce imbarcata

landing capsule
la capsula spaziale

scientist
lo scienziato

control panel
il pannello di controllo

ladder
la scala a pioli

lab coat
il camice

satellite
il satellite

space station
la stazione spaziale

microscope
il microscopio

solar panel
il pannello solare

computer
il computer

spaceship
l'astronave

meteor shower
la pioggia dei meteori

beaker
l'alambicco

alien
l'extraterreste

antenna
l'antenna

constellation
la costellazione

test tube
la provetta

asteroid
l'asteroide

solar system
il sistema solare

galaxy
la galassia

Earth
la Terra

the moon
la luna

the sun
il sole

planet
il pianeta

rings
i circoli

crater
il cratere

stars
le stelle

comet
la cometa

nebula
la nebulosa

rocket
il missile

robot
il robot

24. Human History
La Storia Umana

rock
la roccia

boulder
il masso

bone
l'osso

insect
l'insetto

fern
la felce

tree
l'albero

cave
la caverna

fur
la pelliccia

fire
il fuoco

stick
il bastoncino

wheel
la ruota

flint
la selce

arrowhead
**la punta
di freccia**

club
il bastone

spear
la lancia

mammoth
il mammùt

tusk
la zanna

trunk
la proboscide

bison
il bisonte

paint
il colore

cave drawing
**il disegno
di caverna**

hut
la capanna

corn
il granturco

wheat
il grano

weaver
la tessitrice

loom
il telaio

kiln
la fornace

potter
il vasaio

pot
il vaso

clay
l'argilla

cart
il carro

basket
la cesta

leather
il cuoio

fishing
la pesca

hunter
il cacciatore

well
il pozzo

bucket
la secchia

water
l'acqua

cloth
il panno

saber-toothed tiger
la tigre preistorica

crop
la raccolta

field
il cam

village
il villaggio

cave dwellers
i cavernicoli

skeleton
lo scheletro

dinosaur
il dinosauro

pterodactyl
il pterodattilo

25. The Make-Believe Castle   Il Castello Immaginato

banner
lo stendardo

squire
lo scudiero

court jester
il burlone

dragon
il drago

knight
il cavaliere

minstrel
il menestrello

magic wand
la bacchetta magica

armor
la corazza

unicorn
l'unicorno

fairy
la maga

chain mail
la maglia di ferro

lance
la lancia

elf
l'elfo

forest
la foresta

shield
lo scudo

giant
il gigante

saddle
la sella

ax
l'accetta

forge
la fornace

stirrup
la staffa

sword
la spada

blacksmith
il fabbro ferraio

reins
le briglie

bow
l'arco

anvil
l'incudine

stable
la stalla

arrow
la freccia

horseshoe
il ferro di cavallo

dungeon
il carcere sotterraneo

quiver
la faretra

tower
la torre

moat
il fosso

archer
l'arciere

courtyard
il cortile

castle
il castello

drawbridge
il ponte levatoio

bat
il pipistrello

rat
il ratto

crown
la corona

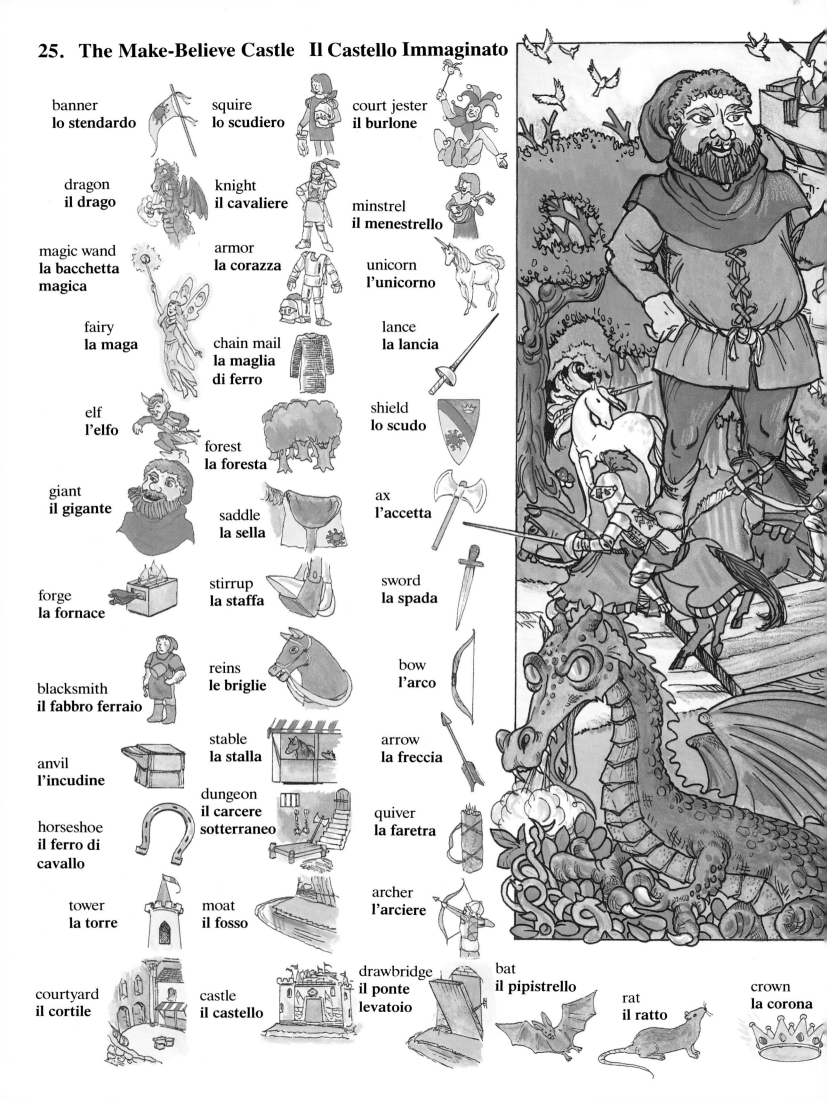

king
il re

queen
la regina

princess
la principessa

prince
il principe

throne
il trono

spider
il ragno

spiderweb
la ragnatela

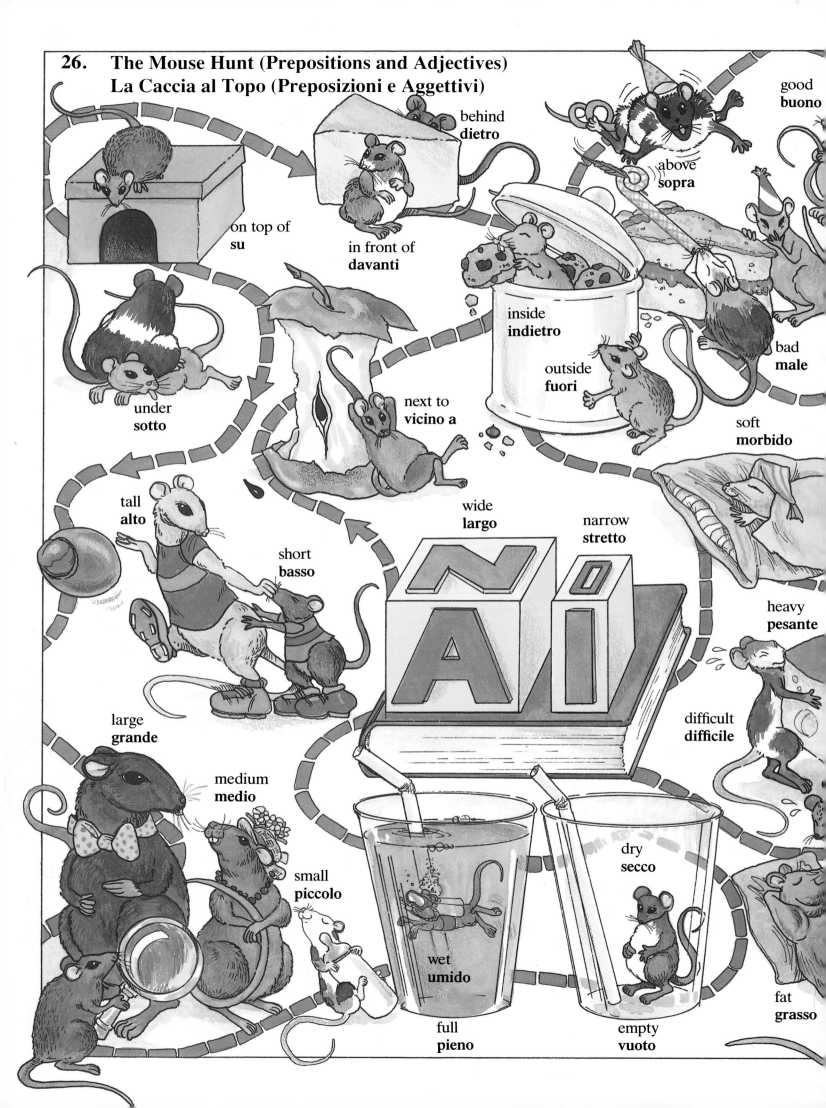

26. The Mouse Hunt (Prepositions and Adjectives)
La Caccia al Topo (Preposizioni e Aggettivi)

good
buono

behind
dietro

above
sopra

on top of
su

in front of
davanti

bad
male

inside
indietro

under
sotto

outside
fuori

soft
morbido

next to
vicino a

tall
alto

wide
largo

narrow
stretto

short
basso

heavy
pesante

large
grande

difficult
difficile

medium
medio

dry
secco

small
piccolo

wet
umido

fat
grasso

full
pieno

empty
vuoto

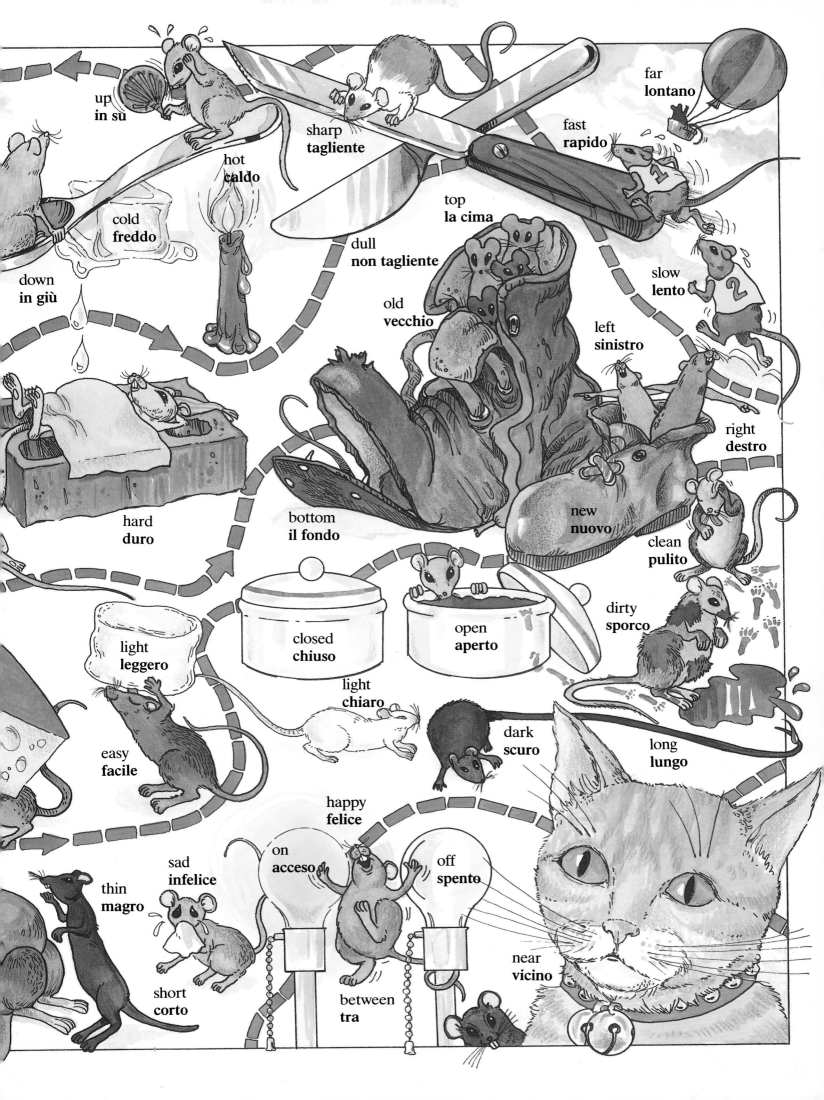

up **in su**

sharp **tagliente**

far **lontano**

fast **rapido**

hot **caldo**

cold **freddo**

top **la cima**

dull **non tagliente**

slow **lento**

down **in giù**

old **vecchio**

left **sinistro**

right **destro**

hard **duro**

bottom **il fondo**

new **nuovo**

clean **pulito**

light **leggero**

closed **chiuso**

open **aperto**

dirty **sporco**

easy **facile**

light **chiaro**

dark **scuro**

long **lungo**

happy **felice**

sad **infelice**

on **acceso**

off **spento**

thin **magro**

short **corto**

between **tra**

near **vicino**

27. Action Words   Le Attività

to drink
bere

to eat
mangiare

to sleep
dormire

to wash (oneself)
lavarsi

to skate
pattinare

to fall
cadere

to cry
piangere

to laugh
ridere

to fly
volare

to write
scrivere

to read
leggere

to play (a game)
giocare

to play (an instrument)
suonare

to sit down
sedersi

to stand up
alzarsi in piedi

to dance
ballare

to walk
camminare

to run
correre

to climb
salire

to jump
saltare

to drive
guidare

to push
spingere

to sell
vendere

to buy
comprare

to ski
sciare

to dive
tuffare

to swim
nuotare

to paint
dipingere

to draw
disegnare

to ride a bicycle
andare a bicicletta

to come **venire**

to go **andare**

to throw **gettare**

to catch **prendere**

to watch **guardare**

to sing **cantare**

to talk **parlare**

to kick **dare un calcio**

to listen (to) **ascoltare**

to think **pensare**

to roar **ruggire**

to dig **scavare**

to water **innaffiare**

to juggle **fare giochi**

to point (at) **mostrare**

to look for **cercare**

to find **trovare**

to give **dare**

to receive **ricevere**

to cut **tagliare**

to cook **cucinare**

to open **aprire**

to close **chiudere**

to take a bath **bagnarsi**

to teach **insegnare**

to break **rompere**

to fix **aggiustare**

to carry **portare**

to pull **tirare**

to wait **aspettare**

28. Colors Colori

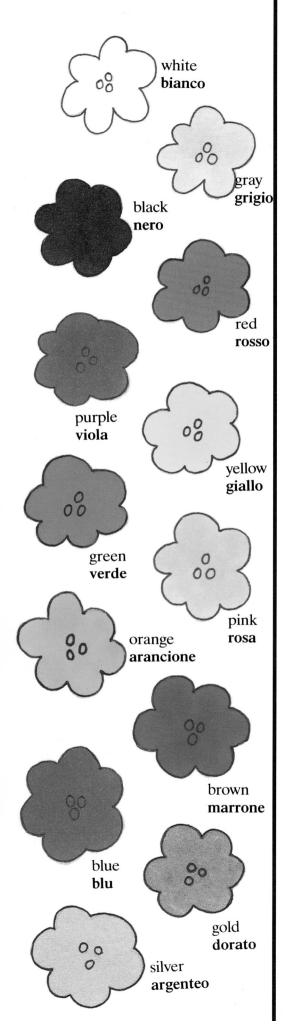

white **bianco**

gray **grigio**

black **nero**

red **rosso**

purple **viola**

yellow **giallo**

green **verde**

pink **rosa**

orange **arancione**

brown **marrone**

blue **blu**

gold **dorato**

silver **argenteo**

29. The Family Tree L'Albero di Famiglia

grandmother, grandma **la nonna**

father, dad **il padre** **il babbo**

mother, mom **la madre** **la mamma**

son **il figlio**

brother **il fratello**

sister **la sorella**

grandfather, grandpa
il nonno

uncle
lo zio

aunt
la zia

cousin
il cugino

cousin
la cugina

daughter
la figlia

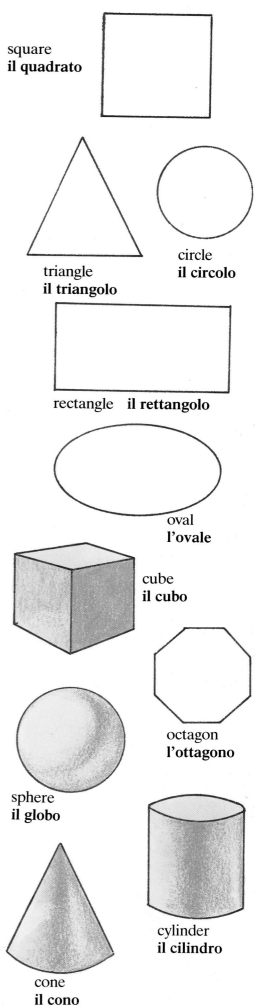

square
il quadrato

triangle
il triangolo

circle
il circolo

rectangle   **il rettangolo**

oval
l'ovale

cube
il cubo

octagon
l'ottagono

sphere
il globo

cylinder
il cilindro

cone
il cono

31. Numbers   I Numeri

Ordinal Numbers
I Numeri Ordinali

tenth **decimo**

ninth **nono**

eighth **ottavo**

sixth **sesto**

seventh **settimo**

fourth **quarto**

fifth **quinto**

second **secondo**

third **terzo**

first **primo**

Cardinal Numbers
I Numeri Cardinali

0 zero **lo zero**	½ one-half **una metà**	1 one **uno**	2 two **due**	3 three **tre**	4 four **quattro**	5 five **cinque**	6 six **sei**

16 sixteen **sedici**	17 seventeen **diciassette**	18 eighteen **diciotto**	19 nineteen **diciannove**	20 twenty **venti**	21 twenty-one **ventuno**

28 twenty-eight **ventotto**	29 twenty-nine **ventinove**	30 thirty **trenta**	31 thirty-one **trentuno**

37 thirty-seven **trentasette**	38 thirty-eight **trentotto**	39 thirty-nine **trentanove**	40 forty **quaranta**

46 forty-six **quarantasei**	47 forty-seven **quarantasette**	48 forty-eight **quarantotto**	49 forty-nine **quarantanove**

55 fifty-five **cinquantacinque**	56 fifty-six **cinquantasei**	57 fifty-seven **cinquantasette**	58 fifty-eight **cinquantotto**

64 sixty-four **sessantaquattro**	65 sixty-five **sessantacinque**	66 sixty-six **sessantasei**	67 sixty-seven **sessantasette**

73 seventy-three **settantatrè**	74 seventy-four **settantaquattro**	75 seventy-five **settantacinque**	76 seventy-six **settantasei**

82 eighty-two **ottantadue**	83 eighty-three **ottantatrè**	84 eighty-four **ottantaquattro**	85 eighty-five **ottantacinque**

91 ninety-one **novantuno**	92 ninety-two **novantadue**	93 ninety-three **novantatrè**	94 ninety-four **novantaquattro**

100 one hundred **cento**	1,000 one thousand **mille**	10,000 ten thousand **dieci mila**

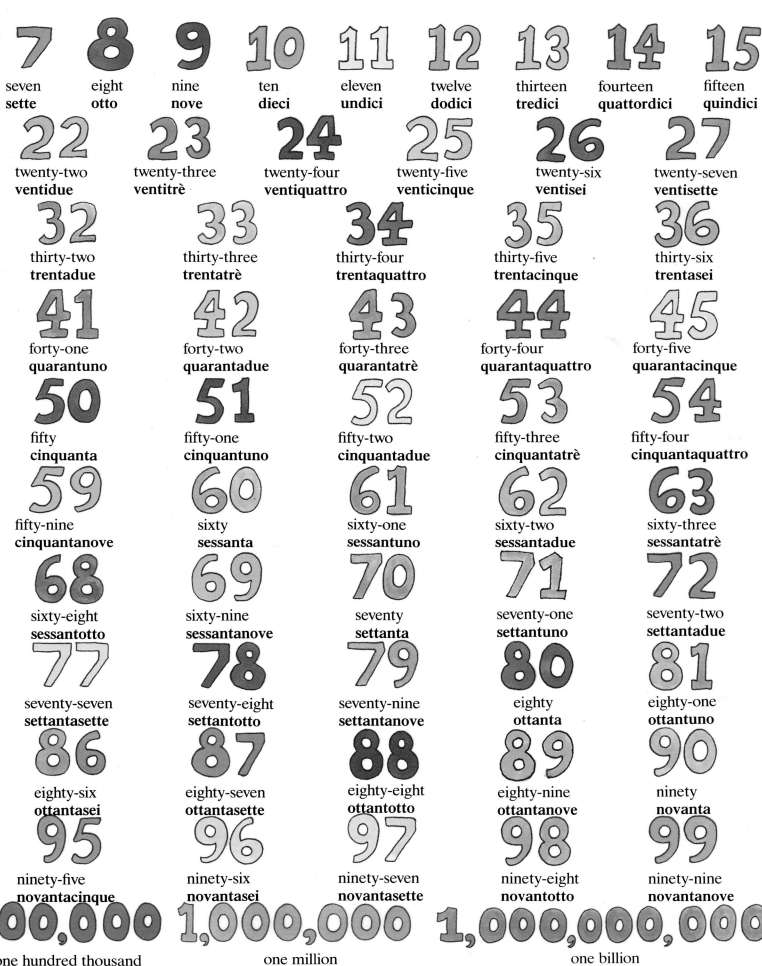

7 seven / sette
8 eight / otto
9 nine / nove
10 ten / dieci
11 eleven / undici
12 twelve / dodici
13 thirteen / tredici
14 fourteen / quattordici
15 fifteen / quindici

22 twenty-two / ventidue
23 twenty-three / ventitrè
24 twenty-four / ventiquattro
25 twenty-five / venticinque
26 twenty-six / ventisei
27 twenty-seven / ventisette

32 thirty-two / trentadue
33 thirty-three / trentatrè
34 thirty-four / trentaquattro
35 thirty-five / trentacinque
36 thirty-six / trentasei

41 forty-one / quarantuno
42 forty-two / quarantadue
43 forty-three / quarantatrè
44 forty-four / quarantaquattro
45 forty-five / quarantacinque

50 fifty / cinquanta
51 fifty-one / cinquantuno
52 fifty-two / cinquantadue
53 fifty-three / cinquantatrè
54 fifty-four / cinquantaquattro

59 fifty-nine / cinquantanove
60 sixty / sessanta
61 sixty-one / sessantuno
62 sixty-two / sessantadue
63 sixty-three / sessantatrè

68 sixty-eight / sessantotto
69 sixty-nine / sessantanove
70 seventy / settanta
71 seventy-one / settantuno
72 seventy-two / settantadue

77 seventy-seven / settantasette
78 seventy-eight / settantotto
79 seventy-nine / settantanove
80 eighty / ottanta
81 eighty-one / ottantuno

86 eighty-six / ottantasei
87 eighty-seven / ottantasette
88 eighty-eight / ottantotto
89 eighty-nine / ottantanove
90 ninety / novanta

95 ninety-five / novantacinque
96 ninety-six / novantasei
97 ninety-seven / novantasette
98 ninety-eight / novantotto
99 ninety-nine / novantanove

100,000 one hundred thousand / cento mila
1,000,000 one million / un milione
1,000,000,000 one billion / un miliardo

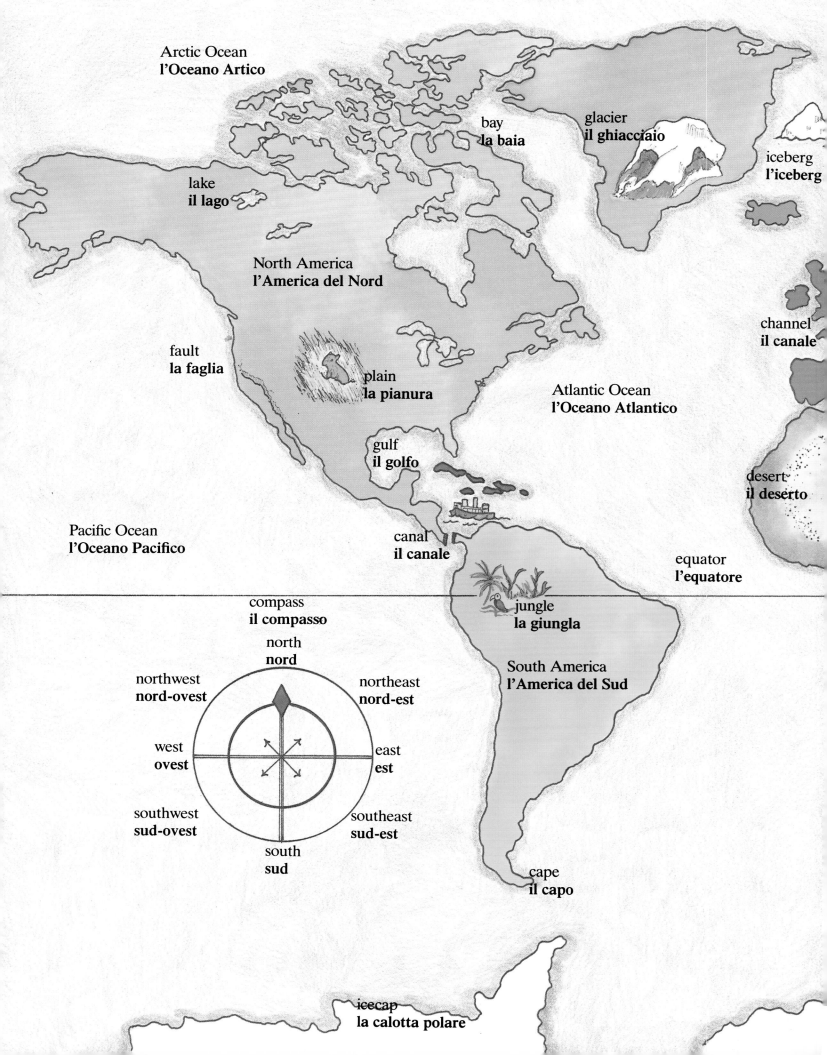

Arctic Ocean
l'Oceano Artico

bay
la baia

glacier
il ghiacciaio

iceberg
l'iceberg

lake
il lago

North America
l'America del Nord

channel
il canale

fault
la faglia

plain
la pianura

Atlantic Ocean
l'Oceano Atlantico

gulf
il golfo

desert
il deserto

Pacific Ocean
l'Oceano Pacifico

canal
il canale

equator
l'equatore

compass
il compasso

jungle
la giungla

north
nord

South America
l'America del Sud

northwest
nord-ovest

northeast
nord-est

west
ovest

east
est

southwest
sud-ovest

southeast
sud-est

south
sud

cape
il capo

icecap
la calotta polare

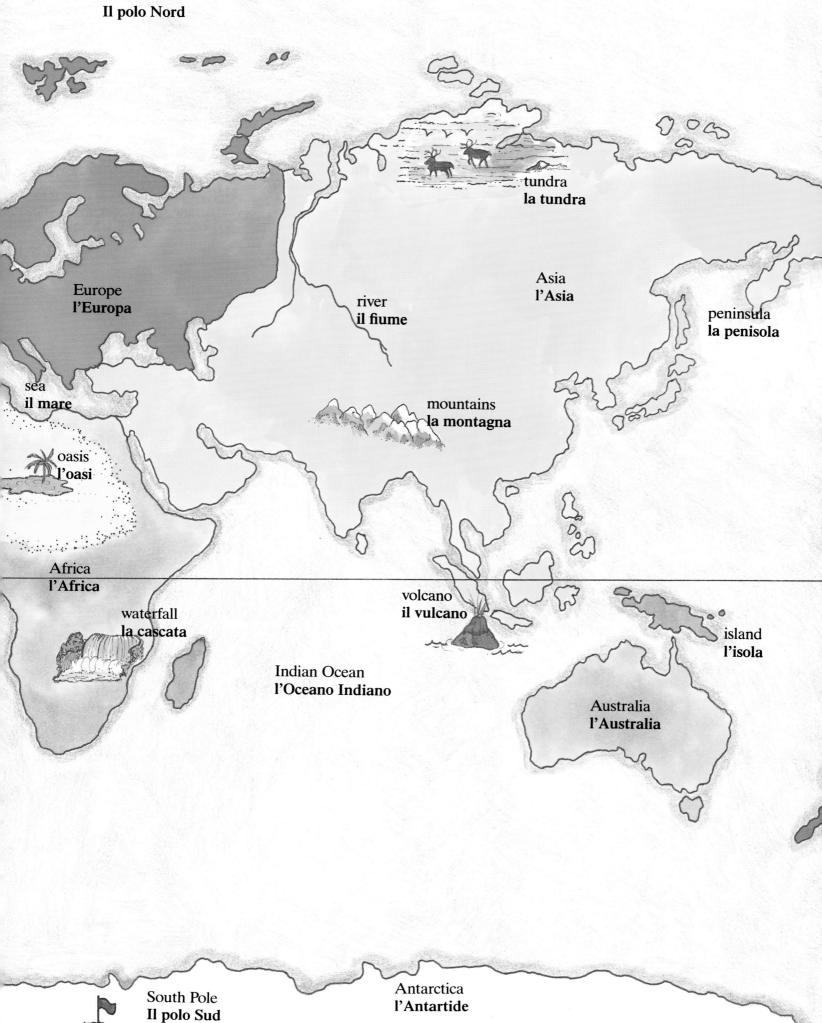

North Pole
Il polo Nord

tundra
la tundra

Asia
l'Asia

river
il fiume

peninsula
la penisola

Europe
l'Europa

sea
il mare

mountains
la montagna

oasis
l'oasi

Africa
l'Africa

waterfall
la cascata

volcano
il vulcano

island
l'isola

Indian Ocean
l'Oceano Indiano

Australia
l'Australia

South Pole
Il polo Sud

Antarctica
l'Antartide

Italian-English Glossary and Index

How to Say the Words in Italian

One of the most difficult things about learning a new language is pronunciation, how to say the words in the language. That's why we've written pronunciation guides to help you say the words in this book correctly. You will find a pronunciation guide in parentheses after each Italian word in the *Italian-English Glossary and Index*. It may look funny, but if you read it aloud, you will be saying the word correctly.

Here are a few hints about saying words in Italian. The Italian *r* is different from the English *r*. To say it correctly, "trill" the sound by flapping your tongue against the roof of your mouth. In Italian, the letter *a* always sounds like the *a* in f*a*ther, the letter *o* always sounds like the *o* in g*o*, and the letter *i* always sounds like the *ee* in f*ee*t. These sounds are written as *ah, oh,* and *ee* in the pronunciation guides. Also, the letter *e* sounds like the *ay* in pl*ay*. This sound is

written as *ay* in the pronunciation guides. Some combinations of letters also have special sounds in Italian. The combination *ai* sounds like the *i* in n*i*ght and is written as *igh* in the pronunciation guides. The combination *au* sounds like the *ow* in n*ow* and is written as *ow* in the pronunciation guides.

You may also notice that each word in the pronunciation guides has one syllable in heavy dark letters. This is the stressed syllable. When you say a word in English, you always say one syllable a little louder than the others. This is called the stressed syllable. When you read the pronunciation guides aloud, just say the syllables in heavy dark letters a little louder than the others to use the correct stress.

After the pronunciation guide, the *Italian-English Glossary and Index* gives the English meaning for each word and the number of the picture where you can find the word.

gli abiti (lyee **ah**-bee-tee), clothing, 7
l'abito nero (**lah**-bee-toh **nay**-roh), tuxedo, 4
l'accappatoio (lah-kahp-pah-**toy**-oh), bathrobe, 7
acceso (ah-**chay**-zoh), on, 26
l'accetta (lah-**chayt**-tah), ax, 25
l'acqua (**lah**-kwah), water, 24
l'acquaio (lah-**kwigh**-oh), sink, 3
l'acquario (lah-**kwah**-ree-oh), aquarium, 1
l'acrobata (lah-kroh-**bah**-tah), acrobat, 21
l'aereo (lah-**ay**-ray-oh), airplane, 16, 17
l'aeroporto (lah-ay-roh-**por**-toh), airport, 17
l'Africa (**lah**-free-kah), Africa, 32
l'agente doganale (lah-**jayn**-tay doh-gah-**nah**-lay), customs officer, 17
gli aggettivi (lyee ahj-jayt-**tee**-vee), adjectives, 26
aggiustare (ahj-joo-**stah**-ray), fix, 27
l'aggraffatrice (lahg-grahf-fah-**tree**-chay), stapler, 1
l'agnello (lahn-**yay**-loh), lamb, 9
l'ago (**lah**-goh), hypodermic needle, 11
l'agricoltore (lah-gree-kohl-**toh**-ray), farmer, 9
l'aiuola (ligh-oo-**oh**-lah), flowerbed, 5
l'ala (**lah**-lah), wing, 17
l'alambicco (lah-lahm-**beek**-koh), beaker, 23
l'albergo (lahl-**bayr**-goh), hotel, 8
l'albero (**lahl**-bay-roh), tree, 9, 24
l'albero di famiglia (**lahl**-bay-roh dee fah-**mee**-lyah), family tree, 29
l'album di fotografie (lahl-**boom** dee foh-toh-grah-**fee**-ay), photo album, 4
l'alfabeto (lahl-fah-**bay**-toh), alphabet, 1
l'alga marina (**lahl**-gah mah-**ree**-nah), seaweed, 22
le ali (lay **ah**-lee), wings, 20
l'aliante (lah-lee-**ahn**-tay), hang glider, 16
l'altalena (lahl-tah-**lay**-nah), swings, 8
alto (**ahl**-toh), tall, 26
l'altoparlante (lahl-toh-par-**lahn**-tay), loudspeaker, 1
l'alunna (lah-**loon**-nah), student (female), 1
l'alunno (lah-**loon**-noh), student (male), 1
alzarsi in piedi (al-**tsahr**-see een pee-**ay**-dee), stand up, 27
l'amaca (lah-**mah**-kah), hammock, 5
l'America del Nord (lah-**may**-ree-kah dayl nord), North America, 32
l'America del Sud (lah-**may**-ree-kah dayl sood), South America, 32

l'amo (**lah**-moh), fishhook, 22
l'ananas (lah-**nahn**-ahz), pineapple, 6
l'anatroccolo (lah-nah-**trohk**-koh-loh), duckling, 9
l'ancora (**lahn**-koh-rah), anchor, 22
andare (ahn-**dah**-ray), go, 27
andare a bicicletta (ahn-**dah**-ray ah bee-chee-**klayt**-tah), ride a bicycle, 27
l'andare a vela (lahn-**dah**-ray ah **vay**-lah), sailing, 18
l'anello (lah-**nayl**-loh), ring, 7
l'angolo (**lahn**-goh-loh), corner, 8
gli animali (lyee ah-nee-**mah**-lee), animals, 20
l'anitra (**lah**-nee-trah), duck, 9
l'Antartide (lahn-**tahr**-tee-day), Antarctica, 32
l'antenna (lahn-**tay**-nah), antenna, 23
l'anticamera (lahn-tee-**kah**-may-rah), waiting room, 11
aperto (ah-**payr**-toh), open, 26
le api (lay **ah**-pee), bees, 9
l'apparecchio per denti (lahp-pah-**ray**-kee-oh payr **dayn**-tee), braces, 11
aprire (ah-**pree**-ray), open, 27
l'aquila (**lah**-kwee-lah), eagle, 20
l'aquilone (lah-kwee-**loh**-nay), kite, 5
le arachidi (lay ah-**rah**-kee-dee), peanuts, 21
l'aragosta (lah-rah-**goh**-stah), lobster, 22
l'arancia (lah-**rahn**-chah), orange, 6
arancione (ah-rahn-**choh**-nay), orange, 28
l'arbitro (**lahr**-bee-troh), referee, umpire, 18
l'archetto (lahr-**kayt**-toh), bow, 19
l'architetto (lahr-kee-**tayt**-toh), architect, 15
l'arciere (lahr-**chay**-ray), archer, 25
l'arco (**lahr**-koh), bow, 25
l'arcobaleno (lahr-koh-bah-**lay**-noh), rainbow, 5
l'arena (lah-**ray**-nah), ring, 21
argenteo (ahr-**jayn**-tay-oh), silver, 28
l'argento (lahr-**jayn**-toh), silver, 22
l'argilla (lahr-**jeel**-lah), clay, 24
l'armadietto farmaceutico (lahr-mah-dee-**ayt**-toh fahr-mah-chay-**oo**-tee-koh), medicine cabinet, 2
l'armadio a muro (lahr-**mah**-dee-oh ah **moo**-roh), closet, 2
l'arpa (**lahr**-pah), harp, 19
l'artiglio (lahr-**tee**-lyoh), claws, 20
l'artista (lahr-**tee**-stah), artist, 15

l'ascensore (lah-shayn-**soh**-ray), elevator, 17
l'asciugacapelli (lah-shyoo-gah-kah-**pay**-lee), hair dryer, 12
l'asciugamani di carta (lah-shyoo-gah-**mah**-nee dee **kahr**-tah), paper towels, 3
l'asciugamano (lah-shyoo-gah-**mah**-noh), towel, 2
l'asciugatrice (lah-shyoo-gah-**tree**-chay), clothes dryer, 3
ascoltare (ah-skohl-**tah**-ray), listen (to), 27
l'Asia (**lah**-zee-ah), Asia, 32
l'asino (**lah**-zee-noh), donkey, 9
aspetta (ah-**spayt**-tah), wait!, 16
aspettare (ah-spayt-**tah**-ray), wait, 27
l'aspirapolvere (lah-spee-rah-**pohl**-vay-ray), vacuum cleaner, 3
l'assegno (lahs-**say**-nyoh), check, 13
l'assistente del dentista (lahs-see-**stayn**-tay dayl dayn-**tee**- stah), dental hygienist, 11
l'assistente del medico (lahs-see-**stayn**-tay dayl **may**-dee-koh), paramedic, 15
l'assistente di volo (lahs-see-**stayn**-tay dee **voh**-loh), flight attendant, 17
l'asta della tenda (**lah**-stah **dayl**-lah **tayn**-dah), tent pole, 21
l'asteroide (lah-stay-**roy**-day), asteroid, 23
l'astronauta (lah-stroh-**now**-tah), astronaut, 23
l'astronave (lah-stroh-**nah**-vay), spaceship, 23
l'astronomo (lah-**stroh**-noh-moh), astronomer, 15
l'atleta (laht-**lay**-tah), athlete, 15
l'attaccapanni (laht-tahk-kah-**pahn**-nee), hanger, 2
le attività (lay aht-tee-vee-**tah**), actions, 27
l'attore (laht-**toh**-ray), actor, 19
l'attrezzo ginnico (laht-**tray**-tsoh **jeen**-nee-koh), jungle gym, 8
l'attrice (laht-**tree**-chay), actress, 19
l'auditorio (low-dee-**toh**-ree-oh), auditorium, 19
l'Australia (low-**strah**-lee-ah), Australia, 32
l'autobus (**low**-toh-boos), bus, 16
l'autobus per scuola (**low**-toh-boos payr **skwoh**-lah), school bus, 16
l'autocisterna (low-toh-chee-**stayr**-nah), tank truck, 14
l'autolavaggio (low-toh-lah-**vahj**-joh), car wash, 14

l'autopompa (low-toh-**pohm**-pah), fire engine, 16

l'autorespiratore (low-toh-ray-spee-rah-**toh**-ray), oxygen tank, 22

l'autunno (low-**toon**-noh), fall, 5

avanti (ah-**vahn**-tee), go!, 16

l'aviorimessa (lah-vee-oh-ree-**mays**-sah), hangar, 17

l'avocado (lah-voh-**kah**-doh), avocado, 6

l'avvocatessa (lahv-voh-kah-**tays**-sah), lawyer, 15

il babbo (eel **bahb**-boh), dad, 29

la bacchetta magica (lah bahk-**kayt**-tah **mah**-jee-kah), magic wand, 25

la bacheca (lah bah-**kay**-kah), bulletin board, 1

i baffi (ee **bahf**-fee), mustache, 12

bagnarsi (bah-**nyahr**-see), take a bath, 27

la baia (la **bigh**-ah), bay, 32

il balcone (eel bahl-**koh**-nay), balcony, 8

la balena (lah bah-**lay**-nah), whale, 22

ballare (bahl-**lah**-ray), dance, 27

la ballerina (lah bahl-lay-**ree**-nah), dancer, 19

la bambola (lah **bahm**-boh-lah), doll, 4

la banana (lah bah-**nah**-nah), banana, 6

la banca (lah **bahn**-kah), bank, 13

il banchiere (eel bahn-**kyay**-ray), banker, 15

il banco (eel **bahn**-koh), counter, 3; pupil desk, 1; school (of fish), 22

il banco corallifero (eel **bahn**-koh koh-rahl-**lee**-fay-roh), coral reef, 22

il bancomat (eel **bahn**-koh-maht), automatic teller, 13

la banda (lah **bahn**-dah), band, 21

le bandiere (lay bahn-**dyay**-ray), flags, 17

la barba (lah **bahr**-bah), beard, 12

il barbiere (eel bahr-**byay**-ray), barber, 12

dal barbiere (dahl bahr-**byay**-ray), barber shop, 12

la barca a remi (lah **bahr**-kah ah **ray**-mee), rowboat, 16

la barca a vela (lah **bahr**-kah ah **vay**-lah), sailboat, 16

la barca (lah **bahr**-kah), boat, 16

il baseball (eel **bah**-zay-bahl), baseball, 18

basso (**bahs**-soh), short, 26

il bastoncino (eel bah-stohn-**chee**-noh), stick, 24

il bastone (eel bah-**stoh**-nay), cane, 11; club, 24

il battone (eel baht-**toh**-nay), baton, 21

il baule (eel **bow**-lay), trunk, 4

la bavella (lah bah-**vayl**-lah), dental floss, 11

il becco (eel **bayk**-koh), beak, 20

il bendaggio a fionda (eel bayn-**dahj**-joh ah fee-**ohn**-dah), sling, 11

bere (**bay**-ray), drink, 27

la betoniera (lah bay-tohn-ee-**ay**-rah), cement mixer, 16

la bevanda (lah bay-**vahn**-dah), soft drink, 10

la biancheria intima (lah bee-ahn-kay-**ree**-ah **een**-tee-mah), underwear, 7

bianco (bee-**ahn**-koh), white, 28

il bibliotecario (eel beeb-lee-oh-tay-**kah**-ree-oh), librarian, 15

il bicchiere (eel beek-kee-**ay**-ray), glass, 10

la bicicletta (lah bee-chee-**klayt**-tah), bicycle, 14, 16, 18

il bigliettaio (eel beel-yay-**tigh**-oh), ticket agent, 17

la biglietteria (lah beel-yayt-tay-**ree**-ah), ticket booth, 21

i biglietti (eel beel-**yayt**-tee), tickets, 21

il biglietto (eel beel-**yayt**-toh), bill, 13; ticket, 17

i bigodini (ee bee-goh-**dee**-nee), curlers, 12

la bilancia (lah bee-**lahn**-chah), scale, 6, 13

il binocolo (eel bee-**noh**-koh-loh), binoculars, 17

biondi (bee-**ohn**-dee), blond, 12

i biscotti (ee bee-**skoht**-tee), cookies, 6

il bisonte (eel bee-**zohn**-tay), bison, 24

la bistecca (lah bee-**stayk**-kah), steak, 10

i blocchi (ee **bloh**-kee), blocks, 4

il blocco (eel **blohk**-koh), notepad, 13

blu (bloo), blue, 28

la bocca di accesso (lah **bohk**-kah dee ah-**chays**-soh), manhole cover, 8

la bocca (lah **boh**-kah), mouth, 11

il boccaglio (eel bohk-**kahl**-yoh), snorkel, 22

il bollitore (eel bohl-lee-**toh**-ray), kettle, 3

la borsa (lah **bohr**-sah), purse, 17

la borsa per documenti (lah **bohr**-sah payr doh-koo-**mayn**-tee), briefcase, 17

la bottiglia (lah boht-**teel**-yah), bottle, 6

il bottone (eel boht-**toh**-nay), button, 7

il braccialetto (eel brah-chah-**layt**-toh), bracelet, 7

il braccio (eel **brah**-choh), arm, 11

le branchie (lay **brahn**-kee-ay), gills, 22

le briglie (lay **breel**-yay), reins, 25

i broccoletti (ee brohk-koh-**layt**-tee), broccoli, 10

la buca dell'orchestra (lah **boo**-kah dayl-lohr-**kay**-strah), orchestra pit, 19

il bucato (eel boo-**kah**-toh), laundry, 3

il buco delle lettere (eel **boo**-koh **dayl**-lay **layt**-**tay**-ray), mail slot, 13

buono (boo-**oh**-noh), good, 26

il burlone (eel boor-**loh**-nay), court jester, 25

il burrattino (eel boor-raht-**tee**-noh), puppet, 4

il burro (eel **boor**-roh), butter, 6

la cabina telefonica (lah kah-**bee**-nah tay-lay-**foh**-nee-kah), phone booth, 13

la caccia (lah **kah**-chah), hunt, 26

il cacciatore (eel kah-chah-**toh**-ray), hunter, 24

il cacciavite (eel kah-chah-**vee**-tay), screwdriver, 3

il cactus (eel **kahk**-toos), cactus, 1

cadere (kah-**day**-ray), fall, 27

il caffè (eel kahf-**fay**), coffee, 10

il calamaro (eel kah-lah-**mah**-roh), squid, 22

il calcio (eel **kahl**-choh), soccer, 18

il calcolatore (eel kahl-koh-lah-**toh**-ray), calculator, 1

caldo (**kahl**-doh), hot, 26

il calendario (eel kah-layn-**dah**-ree-oh), calendar, 1

la calotta polare (lah kah-**loht**-tah poh-**lah**-ray), icecap, 32

calvo (**kahl**-voh), bald, 12

la calzamaglia (lah kahl-tsah-**mahl**-yah), leotard, 19; tights, 7

i calzini (ee kahl-**tsee**-nee), socks, 7

i calzoncini corti (ee kahl-tsohn-**chee**-nee **kohr**-tee), shorts, 7

la camera da letto (lah **kah**-may-rah dah **layt**-toh), bedroom, 2

la cameriera (lah kah-may-ree-**ay**-rah), waitress, 10

il cameriere (eel kah-may-ree-**ay**-ray), waiter, 10

il camerino (eel kah-may-**ree**-noh), dressing room, 19

il camice (eel kah-**mee**-chay), lab coat, 23

la camicetta (lah kah-mee-**chayt**-tah), blouse, 7

la camicia (lah kah-**mee**-chah), shirt, 7

il camino (eel kah-**mee**-noh), chimney, 2

il camion (eel kah-mee-**ohn**), truck, 16

il camionista (eel kah-mee-oh-**nee**-stah), truck driver, 14

il cammello (eel kahm-**mayl**-loh), camel, 20

camminare (kahm-mee-**nah**-ray), walk, 27

la campanella (lah kahm-pah-**nayl**-lah), bell, 1

il camper (eel **kahm**-payr), camper, 16

il campo (eel **kahm**-poh), field, 24

il canale (eel kah-**nah**-lay), canal, 32; channel, 32

il cancellino (eel kahn-chayl-**lee**-noh), eraser (chalkboard), 1

la candela (lah kahn-**day**-lah), candle, 10

il cane (eel **kah**-nay), dog, 9

il canguro (eel kahn-**goo**-roh), kangaroo, 20

il cannone (eel kahn-**noh**-nay), cannon, 22

la cannuccia (lah kahn-**noo**-chah), straw, 10

la canoa (lah kah-**noh**-ah), canoe, 16

il cantante (eel kahn-**tahn**-tay), singer, 19

cantare (kahn-**tah**-ray), sing, 27

la capanna (lah kah-**pahn**-nah), hut, 24

i capelli (ee kah-**payl**-lee), hair, 12

il capo (eel **kah**-poh), cape, 32

il capomastro (eel kah-poh-**mah**-stroh), foreman, 15

il cappello (eel kahp-**payl**-loh), hat, 4, 7

il cappello a cilindro (eel kahp-**payl**-loh ah chee-**leen**-droh), top hat, 4

il cappello da sci (eel kahp-**payl**-loh dah shee), cap, 7

il cappello di cowboy (eel kahp-**payl**-loh dee **kow**-boy), cowboy hat, 4

il cappotto (eel kahp-**poht**-toh), coat, 7

il cappuccio (eel kahp-**poo**-choh), hood, 7

la capra (lah **kah**-prah), goat, 9

il capretto (eel kah-**prayt**-toh), kid, 9

la capsula spaziale (lah **kahp**-soo-lah spah-tsee-**ah**-lay), landing capsule, 23

le caramelle (lay kah-rah-**mayl**-lay), candy, 6

il carcere (eel **kahr**-chay-ray), jail, 8

il carcere sotterraneo (eel **kahr**-chay-ray soht-tayr-**rah**-nay-oh), dungeon, 25

la carne (lah **kahr**-nay), meat, 6

le carote (lay kah-**roh**-tay), carrots, 6

il carrello (eel kahr-**rayl**-loh), shopping cart, 6

il carrello d'atterraggio (eel kahr-**rayl**-loh daht-tayr-**rahj**-joh), landing gear, 17

il carrello per bagagli (eel kahr-**rayl**-loh payr bah-**gah**-lyee), baggage cart, 17

il carro (eel **kahr**-roh), cart, 24

il carro attrezzi (eel **kahr**-roh aht-**tray**-tsee), tow truck, 14

la carrozzina (lah kahr-roh-**tsee**-nah), baby carriage, 16

la carta (lah **kahr**-tah), paper, 1

la carta di credito (lah **kahr**-tah dee **kray**-dee-toh), credit card, 13

la carta geografica (lah **kahr**-tah jay-oh-**grah**-fee-kah), map, 1

la carta igienica (lah **kahr**-tah ee-**jay**-nee-kah), toilet paper, 2

la carta vetrata (lah **kahr**-tah vay-**trah**-tah), sandpaper, 3

le carte (lay **kahr**-tay), cards, 4

le carte di musica (lay **kahr**-tay dee **moo**-zee-kah), sheet music, 19

il cartellino (eel kahr-tayl-**lee**-noh), sign, 6

il cartellone (el kahr-tayl-**loh**-nay), poster, 2

la cartolina (lah kahr-toh-**lee**-nah), postcard, 13

la casa da bambole (lah **kah**-zah dah **bahm**-boh-lay), dollhouse, 4

la casa (lah **kah**-zah), house, 2

la cascata (lah kah-**skah**-tah), waterfall, 32

la cassa (lah **kahs**-sah), cash register, 6

la cassaforte (lah kahs-sah-**fohr**-tay), safe, 13

il cassetone (eel kahs-say-**toh**-nay), treasure chest, 22

la cassetta (lah kahs-**sayt**-tah), cassette tape, 2

la cassetta di sicurezza (lah kahs-**sayt**-tah dee see-koo-**ray**- tsah), safety deposit box, 13

la cassetta per imbucare (lah kahs-**sayt**-tah payr eem-boo-**kah**- ray), post-office box, 13

la cassetta postale (lah kahs-**sayt**-tah poh-**stah**-lay), mailbox, 13

il cassettino (eel kahs-sayt-tee-noh), drawer, 3

la cassiere (lah kahs-see-**ay**-ray), cashier, 6

il cassiere (eel kahs-see-**ay**-ray), teller, 13

castagni (kah-**stan**-yee), brown, 12

il castello (eel kah-**stayl**-loh), castle, 25

la catena (lah kah-**tay**-nah), bicycle chain, 14

la cattedra (lah kaht-**tay**-drah), teacher's desk, 1

il cavaliere (eel kah-vahl-**yay**-ray), knight, 25

la cavallerizza senza sella (lah kah-vahl-lay-**ree**-tsah **sayn**-tsah **sayl**-lah), bareback rider, 21

la cavalletta (lah kah-vahl-**layt**-tah), grasshopper, 5

il cavalletto (eel kah-vahl-**layt**-toh), easel, 1; kickstand, 14

il cavallo (eel kah-**vahl**-loh), horse, 9

il cavallo a dondolo (eel kah-**vahl**-loh ah **dohn**-doh-loh), rocking horse, 4

il cavallo di mare (eel kah-**vahl**-loh dee **mah**-ray), sea horse, 22

la caverna (lah kah-**vayr**-nah), cave, 24

i cavernicoli (ee Kah-vayr-**nee**-koh-lee), cave dwellers, 24

la caviglia (lah kah-**vee**-lyah), ankle, 11

il cavolo (eel **kah**-voh-loh), cabbage, 6

il cellofan (eel chayl-loh-**fahn), cellophane tape, 1**

la cena (lah **chay**-nah), dinner, 10

il cencio (eel **chayn**-choh), rag, 14

cento (**chayn**-toh), hundred, 31

cento mila (**chayn**-toh **mee**-lah), hundred thousand, 31

il ceppo (eel **chayp**-poh), log, 5

cercare (chayr-**kah**-ray), look for, 27

il cerchio (eel **chayr**-kee-oh), hoop, 21

i cereali (ee chay-ray-**ah**-lee), cereal, 6

il cerimoniere (eel chay-ree-moh-nee-**ay**-ray), master of ceremonies, 19

la cerniera (lay chayr-nee-**ay**-rah), zipper, 7

il cerotto medicato (eel chay-**roht**-toh may-dee-**kah**-toh), bandage, 11

il cervo (eel **chayr**-voh), deer, 20

il cespuglio (eel chay-**spool**-yoh), bush, 5

la cesta (lah **chay**-stah), basket, 24

il cestino (eel chay-**stee**-noh), wastebasket, 1

il chiappamosche (eel kee-ahp-pah-**moh**-skay), fly swatter, 5

chiaro (kee-**ah**-roh), light, 26

la chiave (lah kee-**ah**-vay), key, 13; wrench, 3

la chiesa (lah kee-**ay**-zah), church, 8

il chignon (eel keen-**yohn**), bun, 12

il chiodo (eel kee-**oh**-doh), nail, 3

la chitarra (lah kee-**tahr**-rah), guitar, 19

chiudere (**kyoo**-day-ray), close, 27

chiuso (**kyoo**-zoh), closed, 26

il cibo (eel **chee**-boh), food, 6

il ciclismo (eel chee-**klee**-zmoh), cycling, 18

il cielo (eel chee-**ay**-loh), sky, 9

il cigno (eel **cheen**-yoh), swan, 20

le ciliege (lay chee-lee-**ay**-jay), cherries, 6

il cilindro (eel chee-**leen**-droh), cylinder, 30

la cima (lah **chee**-mah), top, 26

il cinema (eel **chee**-nay-mah), movie theatre, 8

cinquanta (cheen-**kwahn**-tah), fifty, 31

cinquantacinque (cheen-kwahn-tah-**cheen**-kway), fifty-five, 31

cinquantadue (cheen-kwahn-tah-**doo**-ay), fifty-two, 31

cinquantanove (cheen-kwahn-tah-**noh**-vay), fifty-nine, 31

cinquantaquattro (cheen-kwahn-tah-**kwaht**-troh), fifty-four, 31

cinquantasei (cheen-kwahn-tah-**say**-ee), fifty-six, 31

cinquantasette (cheen-kwahn-tah-**sayt**-tay), fifty-seven, 31

cinquantatrè (cheen-kwahn-tah-**tray**), fifty-three, 31

cinquantotto (cheen-kwahn-tah-**toht**-toh), fifty-eight, 31

cinquantuno (cheen-kwahn-**too**-noh), fifty-one, 31

cinque (**cheen**-kway), five, 31

la cintura (lah cheen-**too**-rah), belt, 7

la cintura di sicurezza (lah cheen-**too**-rah dee see-koo-**ray**-tsah), seat belt, 14

la cioccolata (lah choh-koh-**lah**-tah), chocolate, 6

le cipolle (lay chee-**pohl**-lay), onions, 6

la cipra (lah **chee**-prah), powder, 12

il circo (eel **cheer**-koh), circus, 21

i circoli (ee **cheer**-koh-lee), rings, 23

il circolo (eel **cheer**-koh-loh), circle, 30

la città (lah cheet-**tah**), city, 8

il clarinetto (eel klah-ree-**nayt**-toh), clarinet, 19

la classe (lah **klahs**-say), classroom, 1

il coccodrillo (eel kohk-koh-**dreel**-loh), alligator, 20

il cocomero (eel koh-koh-**may**-roh), watermelon, 6

la coda (lah **koh**-dah), tail, 20

la coda di cavallo (lah **koh**-dah dee kah-**vahl**-loh), ponytail, 12

il codice postale (eel **koh**-dee-chay poh-**stah**-lay), zip code, 13

il cofano (eel **koh**-fah-noh), hood, 14

la colazione (lah koh-lah-tsee-**oh**-nay), breakfast, 10

la colla (lah **kohl**-lah), glue, 1

la collana (lah kohl-**lah**-nah), necklace, 7

la collina (lah kohl-**lee**-nah), hill, 9

il collo (eel **kohl**-loh), collar, 7

il colore (eel koh-**loh**-ray), paint, 1, 24

colori (koh-**loh**-ree), colors, 28

il coltello (eel kohl-**tayl**-loh), knife, 10

la cometa (lah koh-**may**-tah), comet, 23

la commessa (lah kohm-**mays**-sah), saleswoman, 15

il commesso (eel kohm-**mays**-soh), salesman, 15

la communità (lah kohm-moo-nee-**tah**), community, 15

il compact disc (eel kohm-**pahkt** deesk), compact disc, 2

il compasso (eel kohm-**pahs**-soh), compass, 1, 32

il completo (eel kohm-**play**-toh), suit, 7

comprare (kohm-**prah**-ray), buy, 27

il computer (eel kohm-**poo**-tayr), computer, 23

la conchiglia (lah kohn-**keel**-yah), seashell, 22

il Concorde (eel kohn-**kohr**-day), Concorde, 17

il congelatore (eel kohn-jay-lah-**toh**-ray), freezer, 3

il coniglio (eel koh-**neel**-yoh), rabbit, 9

il cono (eel **koh**-noh), cone, 30

il controllore di volo (eel kohn-trohl-**loh**-ray dee **voh**-loh), air-traffic controller, 17

il coperchio del serbatoio (eel koh-**payr**-kee-oh dayl sayr-bah-**toy**-oh), gas cap, 14

la coperta di lana (lah koh-**payr**-tah dee **lah**-nah), blanket, 2

il copione (eel koh-pee-**oh**-nay), script, 19

il coprimozzo (eel koh-pree-**moh**-tsoh), hubcap, 14

il corallo (eel koh-**rahl**-loh), coral, 22

la corazza (lah koh-**rah**-tsah), armor, 25

la corda (lah **kohr**-dah), jump rope, 4; rope, 19, 21; strings, 19

la corda tesa per funamboli (lah **kohr**-dah **tay**-zah payr foo-**nahm**-boh-lee), tightrope, 21

le corna (lay **kohr**-nah), horns, 9, 20

il cornetto (eel kohr-**nayt**-toh), French horn, 19

la cornice (lah kohr-**nee**-chay), picture frame, 4

la corona (lah koh-**roh**-nah), crown, 25

correre (**kohr**-ray-ray), run, 27

il correre (eel **kohr**-ray-ray), running, 18

la corsa (lah **kohr**-sah), car racing, 18

la corsa a ostacoli (lah **kohr**-sah ah oh-**stah**-koh-lee), hurdles, 18

la corsa da cavalli (lah **kohr**-sah dah kah-**vahl**-lee), horse racing, 18

corti (**kohr**-tee), short, 12

il cortile (eel kohr-**tee**-lay), courtyard, 25; yard, 5

corto (**kohr**-toh), short, 26

la costellazione (lah koh-stayl-lah-tsee-**oh**-nay), constellation, 23

il costume (eel koh-**stoo**-may), costume, 19

il costume da bagno (eel koh-**stoo**-may dah **bah**-nyoh), bathing suit, 7

il cowboy (eel **kow**-boy), cowboy, 15

i crackers (ee **krah**-kayrs), crackers, 6

il cratere (eel krah-**tay**-ray), crater, 23

la cravatta (lah krah-**vaht**-tah), tie, 7

la crema da barba (lah **kray**-mah dah **bahr**-bah), shaving cream, 12

il cricco (eel **kreek**-koh), jack, 14

la criniera (lah kree-nee-**ay**-rah), mane, 20

il cristallo di luna (eel kree-**stahl**-loh dee **loo**-nah), moon rock, 23

il cronista (eel kroh-**nee**-stah), reporter, 15

il crostino (eel kroh-**stee**-noh), toast, 10

il cruscotto (eel kroo-**skoht**-toh), dashboard, 14

il cubo (eel **koo**-boh), cube, 30

il cucchiaio (eel kook-kee-**igh**-oh), spoon, 10

il cucciolo (eel koo-**choh**-loh), puppy, 9

la cucina (lah koo-**chee**-nah), kitchen, 2, 3

cucinare (koo-chee-**nah**-ray), cook, 27

la cuffia (lah **koof**-fee-ah), headset, 17

la cugina (lah koo-**jee**-nah), cousin (female), 29

il cugino (eel koo-**jee**-noh), cousin (male), 29

la culla (lah **kool**-lah), cradle, 4

il cuoco (eel koo-**oh**-koh), cook, 15

il cuoio (eel koo-**oy**-oh), leather, 24

i dadi (ee **dah**-dee), dice, 4

dare (**dah**-ray), give, 27

dare un calcio (**dah**-ray oon **kahl**-choh), kick, 27

davanti (dah-**vahn**-tee), in front of, 26

decimo (**day**-chee-moh), tenth, 31

il delfino (eel dayl-**fee**-noh), dolphin, 22

il denaro (eel day-**nahr**-oh), money, 6

il dente (eel **dayn**-tay), tooth, 11

il dentifricio (eel dayn-tee-**free**-choh), toothpaste, 11

il dentista (eel dayn-**tee**-stah), dentist, 11

dal dentista (dahl dayn-**tee**-stah), dentist's office, 11

il deposito bagagli (eel day-**poh**-zee-toh bah-**gahl**-yee), luggage compartment, 17

il deserto (eel day-**zayr**-toh), desert, 32

destro (**day**-stroh), right, 26

il detersivo (eel day-tayr-**see**-voh), laundry
  detergent, 3
diciannove (dee-chah-**noh**-vay), nineteen, 31
diciasette (dee-chah-**sayt**-tay), seventeen, 31
diciotto (dee-**choht**-toh), eighteen, 31
dieci mila (dee-**ay**-chee **mee**-lah), ten thousand,
  31
dieci (dee-**ay**-chee), ten, 31
dietro (dee-**ay**-troh), behind, 26
difficile (dee-fee-chee-lay), difficult, 26
il dinosauro (eel dee-noh-**zow**-roh), dinosaur, 24
dipingere (dee-**peen**-jay-ray), paint, 27
il direttore d'orchestra (eel dee-rayt-**toh**-ray
  dohr-**kay**-strah), conductor, 19
il dirigibile (eel dee-ree-**jee**-bee-lay), blimp, 16
il disc jockey (eel deesk **joh**-kee), disc jockey, 15
il disco (eel **dee**-skoh), record, 2
disegnare (dee-zay-**nyah**-ray), draw, 27
il disegno di caverna (eel dee-**zay**-nyoh dee
  kah-**vayr**-nah), cave drawing, 24
il dito (eel **dee**-toh), finger, 11
il dito del piede (eel **dee**-toh dayl pee-**ay**-day),
  toe, 11
il divano (eel dee-**vah**-noh), sofa, 2
la divisa (lah dee-**vee**-zah), uniform, 4
la doccia (lah **doh**-chah), shower, 2
dodici (**doh**-dee-chee), twelve, 31
il domatore dei leoni (eel doh-mah-**toh**-ray
  day-ee lay-**oh**-nee), lion tamer, 21
la donna (lah **dohn**-nah), woman, 9
la donna poliziotto (lah **dohn**-nah
  poh-lee-tsee-**oht**-toh), policewoman, 15
dorato (doh-**rah**-toh), gold, 28
dormire (dohr-**mee**-ray), sleep, 27
la dottoressa (lah doht-toh-**rays**-sah), doctor, 11
il drago (eel **drah**-goh), dragon, 25
la drogheria (lah droh-gay-**ree**-ah), grocery
  store, 8
due (**doo**-ay), two, 31
duro (**doo**-roh), hard, 26

l'edificio (lay-dee-**fee**-choh), building, 8
l'edificio degli appartamenti (lay-dee-**fee**-choh
  dayl-yee ahp- pahr-tah-**mayn**-tee), apartment
  building, 8
l'elastico (lay-**lah**-stee-koh), rubber band, 13
l'elefante (lay-lay-**fahn**-tay), elephant, 20, 21
l'elettricista (lay-layt-tree-**chee**-stah), electrician,
  15
l'elfo (**layl**-foh), elf, 25
l'elica (**lay**-lee-kah), propeller, 17
l'elicottero (lay-lee-**koht**-tay-roh), helicopter, 16
l'elmetto (layl-**may**-toh), helmet, 18
l'elmo (**layl**-moh), helm, 22
l'elmo spaziale (**layl**-moh spah-tsee-**ah**-lay),
  space helmet, 23
l'equatore (lay-kwah-**toh**-ray), equator, 32
l'equitazione (lay-kwee-tah-tsee-**oh**-nay),
  horseback riding, 18
l'erba (**layr**-bah), grass, 9
est (ayst), east, 32
l'estate (lay-**stah**-tay), summer, 5
l'etichetta (lay-tee-**kayt**-tah), label, 13
l'Europa (lay-oo-**roh**-pah), Europe, 32
l'extraterreste (lay-strah-tayr-**ray**-stay), alien, 23

la fabbrica (lah **fahb**-bree-kah), factory, 8
il fabbro ferraio (eel **fahb**-broh fayr-**righ**-oh),
  blacksmith, 25
il facchino (eel fahk-**kee**-noh), porter, 17
la faccia (lah **fah**-chah), face, 11

facile (**fah**-chee-lay), easy, 26
i fagiolini (ee fah-joh-**lee**-nee), green beans, 6
la faglia (lah **fahl**-yah), fault, 32
la falciatrice meccanica (lah fahl-chah-**tree**-chay
  mak-**kah**-nee- kah), lawn mower, 5
il falegname (eel fah-lay-**nyah**-may), carpenter,
  15
il fanalo (eel fah-**nah**-loh), headlight, 14
il fango (eel **fahn**-goh), mud, 5
fare giochi (**fah**-ray joh-kee), juggle, 27
la faretra (lah fah-**ray**-trah), quiver, 25
la farfalla (lah fahr-**fahl**-lah), butterfly, 5
la farina (lah fah-**ree**-nah), flour, 3
la farmacia (lah fahr-mah-**chee**-ah), drugstore,
  pharmacy, 8
la farmacista (lah fahr-mah-**chee**-stah),
  pharmacist, 15
il faro (eel **fah**-roh), lighthouse, 16
il fascio di luce (eel **fah**-shoh dee **loo**-chay),
  spotlight, 19
la fattoria (lah faht-toh-**ree**-ah), farm, 9
il fazzoletto (eel fah-tsoh-**layt**-toh),
  handkerchief, 7
la felce (lah **fayl**-chay), fern, 24
felice (fay-**lee**-chay), happy, 26
il fenicottero (eel fay-nee-**koht**-tay-roh),
  flamingo, 20
il fermacapelli (eel fayr-mah-kah-**payl**-lee),
  barrette, 12
la fermata (lah fayr-**mah**-tah), bus stop, 16
i ferri da calza (ee **fayr**-ree dah **kahl**-tsah),
  knitting needles, 4
il ferro da stiro (eel **fayr**-roh dah **stee**-roh), iron,
  3
il ferro di cavallo (eel **fayr**-roh dee
  kah-**vahl**-loh), horseshoe, 25
il ferro per arricciare i capelli (eel **fayr**-roh payr
  ahr-ree-**chah**-ray ee kah-**payl**-lee), curling
  iron, 12
la festa di compleanno (lah **fay**-stah dee
  kohm-play-**ahn**-noh), birthday party, 10
i fiammiferi (ee fee-ahm-**mee**-fay-ree), matches,
  5
la fibbia (lah **feeb**-bee-ah), buckle, 7
il fieno (eel fee-**ay**-noh), hay, 9
la figlia (lah **feel**-yah), daughter, 29
il figlio (eel **feel**-yoh), son, 29
la filaccia (lah fee-**lah**-chah), yarn, 4
il filatoio (eel fee-lah-**toy**-oh), spinning wheel, 4
la finestra (lah fee-**nay**-strah), window, 2
il fiocco (eel fee-**ohk**-koh), bow, 13
il fiocco di neve (eel fee-**ohk**-koh dee **nay**-vay),
  snowflake, 5
i fiori (ee fee-**oh**-ree), flowers, 5
la fiorista (lah fee-oh-**ree**-stah), florist, 15
la firma (lah **feer**-mah), signature, 13
la fisarmonica (lah fee-zahr-**moh**-nee-kah),
  accordion, 19
il fiume (eel fee-**oo**-may), river, 32
il flauto (eel **flow**-toh), flute, 19
la foca (lah **foh**-kah), seal, 20
il focolare (eel foh-koh-**lah**-ray), fireplace, 2
la foglia (lah **fohl**-yah), leaf, 5
il fon (eel fohn), blow dryer, 12
il fondo (eel **fohn**-doh), bottom, 26;
  cross-country skiing, 18
la fontana (lah fohn-**tah**-nah), fountain, 8
il food processor (eel food processor), food
  processor, 3
il football americano (eel **foot**-bahl
  ah-may-ree-**kah**-noh), football, 18
il footing (eel **foo**-teeng), jogging, 18
le forbici (lay **fohr**-bee-chee), scissors, 1, 12

la forchetta (lah fohr-**kayt**-tah), fork, 10
la foresta (lah foh-**ray**-stah), forest, 25
il formaggio (eel fohr-**mahj**-joh), cheese, 6
le forme (lay **fohr**-may), shapes, 30
la formica (lah fohr-**mee**-kah), ant, 9
la fornace (lah fohr-**nah**-chay), forge, 25; kiln, 24
il fornello (eel fohr-**nayl**-loh), stove, 3
il forno (eel **fohr**-noh), oven, 3
il forno a microonda (eel **fohr**-noh ah
  mee-kroh-**ohn**-dah), microwave oven, 3
il fosso (eel **fohs**-soh), moat, 25
la foto (lah **foh**-toh), photograph, 4
il fotografo (eel foh-toh-**grah**-foh),
  photographer, 15
le fragole (lay **frah**-goh-lay), strawberries, 6
il francobollo (eel frahn-koh-**bohl**-loh), stamp, 13
la frangia (lah **frahn**-jah), bangs, 12
il fratello (eel frah-**tayl**-loh), brother, 29
la freccia (lah **fray**-chah), arrow, 25
freddo (**frayd**-doh), cold, 26
il freno a mano (eel **fray**-noh ah **mah**-noh), hand
  brake, 14
il frigorifero (eel free-goh-**ree**-fay-roh),
  refrigerator, 3
la frittata (lah freet-**tah**-tah), omelet, 10
la fronte (lah **frohn**-tay), forehead, 11
la frusta (la **froo**-stah), whip, 21
le frutta (lay **froot**-tah), fruit, 6
il fulmine (eel **fool**-mee-nay), lightning, 5
il fumaiolo (eel foo-migh-**oh**-loh), smokestack, 8
il fumo (eel **foo**-moh), smoke, 9
la funambola (lah foo-**nahm**-boh-lah), tightrope
  walker, 21
il fungo (eel **foon**-goh), mushroom, 10
il fuoco (eel foo-**oh**-koh), fire, 24
fuori (foo-**oh**-ree), outside, 26
il furgone (eel foor-**goh**-nay), van, 16

la gabbia (lah **gahb**-bee-ah), cage, 21
i gabinetti (ee gah-bee-**nayt**-tee), rest rooms, 21
la galassia (lah gah-lahs-**see**-ah), galaxy, 23
la gallina (lah gahl-**lee**-nah), hen, 9
il gallo (eel **gahl**-loh), rooster, 9
la gamba (lah **gahm**-bah), leg, 11
il garage (eel gah-**rah**-jay), garage, 14
il gattino (eel gaht-**tee**-noh), kitten, 9
il gatto (eel **gaht**-toh), cat, 9
il gatto delle nevi (eel **gaht**-toh **dayl**-lay
  nay-vee), snowmobile, 5
il gattopardo (eel gaht-toh-**pahr**-doh), leopard,
  20
il gavitello (eel gah-vee-**tayl**-loh), buoy, 22
il gelato (eel jay-**lah**-toh), ice cream, 10
la gente (lah **jayn**-tay), people, 15
il gesso (eel **jays**-soh), cast, 11; chalk, 1
gettare (jayt-**tah**-ray), throw, 27
i ghiacci (ee gee-**ah**-chee), ice cubes, 3
il ghiacciaio (eel gee-ah-**chigh**-oh), glacier, 32
il ghiaccio (eel gee-**ah**-choh), ice, 5
il ghiacciolo (eel gee-ah-**choh**-loh), icicle, 5
la giacca (lah **jahk**-kah), jacket, 7
il giaguaro (eel jah-goo-**ah**-roh), jaguar, 20
giallo (**jahl**-loh), yellow, 28
il giardiniere (eel jahr-deen-ee-**ay**-ray),
  gardener, 15
il gigante (eel jee-**gahn**-tay), giant, 25
il gilè di piuma (eel jee-**lay** dee pee-**oo**-mah),
  down vest, 7
la ginnastica (lah jeen-**nah**-stee-kah),
  gymnastics, 18
il ginocchio (eel jee-**noh**-kee-oh), knee, 11
giocare (johk-**kah**-ray), play (a game), 27

i giocattoli (ee joh-**kaht**-toh-lee), toys, 4

il gioco (eel **joh**-koh), game, 4

il gioco degli scacchi (eel **joh**-koh **dayl**-yee **skah**-kee), chess, 4

il gioco dei birilli automatici (eel **joh**-koh **day**-ee bee-**reel**-lee ow-toh-**mah**-tee-chee), bowling, 18

il gioco della dama (eel **joh**-koh **dayl**-lah **dah**-mah), checkers, 4

il giocoliere (eel joh-koh-lee-**ay**-ray), juggler, 21

il gioielliere (eel joy-ayl-lee-**ay**-ray), jeweler, 15

il gioiello (eel joy-**ayl**-loh), jewel, 22

il giornale (eel johr-**nah**-lay), newspaper, 8

i giornali a fumetti (ee johr-**nah**-lee ah foo-**mayt**-tee), comic books, 4

il giradischi (eel jee-rah-**dee**-skee), record player, 2

la giraffa (lah jee-**rahf**-fah), giraffe, 20

il giudice (eel **joo**-dee-chay), judge, 15

la giungla (lah **joon**-glah), jungle, 32

il globo (eel **gloh**-boh), globe, 1; sphere, 30

la gobba (lah **gohb**-bah), hump, 20

la goccia di pioggia (lah **goh**-chah dee pee-**oh**-jah), raindrop, 5

il golf (eel gohlf), golf, 18; sweater, 7

il golfo (eel **gohl**-foh), gulf, 32

il gomito (eel goh-**mee**-toh), elbow, 11

la gomma (lah **gohm**-mah), eraser (pencil), 1; tire, 14

la gomma a terra (la **gohm**-mah ah **tayr**-rah), flat tire, 14

il goniometro (eel goh-nee-oh-**may**-troh), protractor, 1

la gonna (lah **gohn**-nah), skirt, 7

il gorgoglio (eel gohr-**gohl**-yoh), bubble, 22

il gorilla (eel goh-**reel**-lah), gorilla, 20

la graffa (lah **grahf**-fah), paper clip, 13

le graffette (lay grahf-**fayt**-tay), staples, 1

il granaio (el grah-**nigh**-oh), barn, 9

il granchio (eel **grahn**-chee-oh), crab, 22

grande (**grahn**-day), large, 26

il grano (eel **grah**-noh), wheat, 24

il granturco (eel grahn-**toor**-koh), corn, 24

grasso (**grahs**-soh), fat, 26

il grattacielo (eel graht-tah-**chay**-loh), skyscraper, 8

il grembiale (eel graym-bee-**ah**-lay), apron, 3

grigio (**gree**-joh), gray, 28

la griglia (lah **greel**-yah), barbecue, 5

la gru (lah groo), crane, 8

la gruccia (lah **groo**-chah), crutch, 11

la guancia (lah goo-**ahn**-chah), cheek, 11

il guanciale (eel goo-**ahn**-chah-lay), pillow, 2

i guanti (ee goo-**ahn**-tee), gloves, 7

i guanti a manopola (ee goo-**ahn**-tee ah mah-**noh**-poh-lah), mittens, 7

i guantoni (ee goo-ahn-**toh**-nee), boxing gloves, 18

guardare (goo-ahr-**dah**-ray), watch, 27

la guardia (lah goo-**ahr**-dee-ah), security guard, 13

il gufo (eel **goo**-foh), owl, 20

la guida (lah goo-**ee**-dah), tour guide, 15

guidare (goo-ee-**dah**-ray), drive, 27

il guidatore dell'autobus (eel goo-ee-dah-**toh**-ray dayl **ow**-toh-boos), bus driver, 15

l'hockey (**loh**-kay), hockey, 18

l'iceberg (ligh-**sboorg**), iceberg, 32

l'idrante (lee-**drahn**-tay), fire hydrant, 8; garden hose, 5

l'idraulico (lee-**drow**-lee-koh), plumber, 15

immaginato (eem-mah-jee-**nah**-toh), make-believe, 25

l'impermeabile (leem-payr-may-**ah**-bee-lay), raincoat, 7

l'impiegato dell'ufficio postale (leem-pee-ay-**gah**-toh day-loof-**fee**-choh poh-**stah**-lay), postal worker, 13

in giù (een joo), down, 26

in su (een soo), up, 26

l'incrocio (lee-**kroh**-choh), intersection, 16

l'incudine (leen-**koo**-dee-nay), anvil, 25

indietro (een-dee-**ay**-troh), inside, 26

l'indirizzo (leen-dee-**ree**-tsoh), address, 13

l'indirizzo del mittente (leen-dee-**ree**-tsoh dayl mee-**tayn**-tay), return address, 13

l'indossatrice (leen-dohs-sah-**tree**-chay), model, 15

infelice (een-fay-**lee**-chay), sad, 26

l'infermiere (leen-fayr-mee-**ay**-ray), nurse, 11

innaffiare (een-nahf-fee-**ah**-ray), water, 27

l'insalata (leen-sah-**lah**-tah), salad, 10

insegnare (een-say-**nyah**-ray), teach, 27

l'insetto (leen-**sayt**-toh), insect, 24

l'intasamento (leen-ta-zah-**mayn**-toh), traffic jam, 8

l'inverno (leen-**vayr**-noh), winter, 5

l'ippopotamo (leep-poh-**poh**-tah-moh), hippopotamus, 20

l'isola (lee-**zoh**-lah), island, 32

l'istituto di bellezza (lee-stee-**too**-toh dee bayl-**lay**-tsah), beauty salon, 12

i jeans (ee jeens), jeans, 7

il jeep (eel jeep), jeep, 16

il ketchup (eel ketchup), ketchup, 10

le labbra (lay **lahb**-brah), lips, 11

il laboratorio (eel lah-boh-rah-**toh**-ree-oh), laboratory, 23

il lago (eel **lah**-goh), lake, 32

la lampada (lah **lahm**-pah-dah), lamp, 2

la lampadina (lah lahm-pah-**dee**-nah), lightbulb, 4, 21

la lampadina tascabile (lah lahm-pah-**dee**-nah tah-**skah**-bee-lay), flashlight, 3

i lamponi (ee lahm-**poh**-nee), raspberries, 6

la lancetta (lah lahn-**chayt**-tah), hand, 1

la lancia (lah **lahn**-chah), lance, 25; spear, 24

largo (**lahr**-goh), wide, 26

il latte (eel **laht**-tay), milk, 6

la lattuga (lah laht-**too**-gah), lettuce, 6

la lavagna (lah lah-**vah**-nyah), chalkboard, 1

la lavanderia (lah lah-vahn-day-**ree**-ah), utility room, 3

il lavapiatti (eel lah-vah-pee-**aht**-tee), dishwasher, 3

lavarsi (lah-**vahr**-see), wash (oneself), 27

la lavatrice (lah lah-vah-**tree**-chay), washing machine, 3

leggere (**layj**-jay-ray), read, 27

leggero (layj-**jay**-roh), light, 26

il legno (eel **lay**-nyoh), wood, 3

le lentiggini (lay layn-**teej**-jee-nee), freckles, 12

lento (**layn**-toh), slow, 26

la lenza (lah **layn**-zah), fishing line, 22

il lenzuolo (eel layn-zoo-**oh**-loh), sheet, 2

il leone (eel lay-**oh**-nay), lion, 20, 21

la lettera (lah **layt**-tay-rah), letter, 13

il letto (eel **layt**-toh), bed, 2

la libreria (lah lee-bray-**ree**-ah), bookstore, 8

il libretto d'assegni (eel lee-**brayt**-toh dahs-**say**-nyee), checkbook, 13

il libro (eel **lee**-broh), book, 1

il libro di disegni (eel **lee**-broh dee dee-**zay**-nyee), coloring book, 4

la lima (lah **lee**-mah), file, 3

la limaiola (lah lee-migh-**oh**-lah), nail file, 12

il limone (eel lee-**moh**-nay), lemon, 6

la lingua (lah **leen**-goo-ah), tongue, 11

lisci (**lee**-shee), straight, 12

lontano (lohn-**tah**-noh), far, 26

la lotta sportiva (lah **loht**-tah spohr-**tee**-vah), wrestling, 18

la lucertola (lah loo-**chayr**-toh-lah), lizard, 20

le luci dei freni (lay **loo**-chee **day**-ee **fray**-nee), brake lights, 14

la luna (lah **loo**-nah), moon, 23

lunghi (**loon**-gee), long, 12

lungo (**loon**-goh), long, 26

il lupo (eel **loo**-poh), wolf, 20

il lupo di mare (eel **loo**-poh dee **mah**-ray), barnacle, 22

le macchie (lay **mahk**-kee-ay), spots, 20

la macchina (lah **mahk**-kee-nah), car, 16

la macchina da corsa (lah **mahk**-kee-nah dah **kohr**-sah), race car, 14

la macchina da polizia (lah **mahk**-kee-nah dah poh-lee-**tsee**-ah), police car, 16

la macchina da scrivere (lah **mahk**-kee-nah dah skree-**vay**-ray), typewriter, 13

la macchina fotografica (lah **mahk**-kee-nah foh-toh-**grah**-fee-kah), camera, 17, 21

la macchina lunare (lah **mahk**-kee-nah loo-**nah**-ray), lunar rover, 23

la macchina per cucire (lah **mahk**-kee-nah payr koo-**chee**-ray), sewing machine, 19

il macellaio (eel mah-chay-**ligh**-oh), butcher, 15

la macelleria (lah mah-chayl-lay-**ree**-ah), butcher shop, 8

la madre (lah **mah**-dray), mother, 29

la maestra (lah mah-**ay**-strah), teacher (female), 1

il maestro (eel mah-**ay**-stroh), teacher (male), 1

la maga (lah **mah**-gah), fairy, 25

la maglia di ferro (lah **mahl**-yah dee **fayr**-roh), chain mail, 25

la maglietta (lah mahl-**yayt**-tah), T-shirt, 7

la maglietta sportiva (lah mahl-**yayt**-tah spohr-**tee**-vah), sweatshirt, 7

il magnete (eel mah-**nyay**-tay), magnet, 4

il magnetofono (eel mah-nyay-**toh**-foh-noh), cassette player, 2

il mago (eel **mah**-goh), magician, 21

magro (**mah**-groh), thin, 26

il maiale (eel migh-**ah**-lay), pig, 9

male (**mah**-lay), bad, 26

la mamma (lah **mahm**-mah), mom, 29

il mammùt (eel mahm-**moot**), mammoth, 24

mangiare (mahn-**jah**-ray), eat, 27

la manica (lah **mah**-nee-kah), sleeve, 7

il manicotto dell'aria (eel mah-nee-**koht**-toh dayl-**lah**-ree-ah), air hose, 14

la manicure (lah mah-nee-**koo**-ray), manicurist, 12

la maniglia (lah mah-**neel**-yah), door handle, 14

la mano (lah **mah**-noh), hand, 11

il manovale (eel mah-noh-vah-**lay**), construction worker, 15

la mantellina (lah mahn-tayl-**lee**-nah), cape, 21

il manubrio di bicicletta (eel **mah-noo**-bree-oh dee bee-chee-**klayt**-tah), handlebars, 14

il marciapiede (eel mahr-chah-pee-**ay**-day), sidewalk, 16

il mare (eel **mah**-ray), sea, 32

il marinaio (eel mah-ree-**nigh**-oh), sailor, 15

la marmellata (lah mahr-mayl-**lah**-tah), jam, 10

marrone (mahr-**roh**-nay), brown, 28

il martello (eel mahr-**tayl**-loh), hammer, 3

la mascara (lah **mah**-skah-rah), mascara, 12

la maschera (lah **mah**-skay-rah), mask, 19, 22

il masso (eel **mahs**-soh), boulder, 24

la matita (lah **mah**-tee-tah), pencil, 1

le matite colorate (lay mah-**tee**-tay koh-loh-**rah**-tay), colored pencils, 1

il mattone (eel maht-**toh**-nay), brick, 3

la mazza (lah **mah**-tsah), bat, 18

la mazza da golf (lah **mah**-tsah dah gohlf), golf club, 18

il meccanico (eel mayk-**kah**-nee-koh), mechanic, 14

la medaglia (lah may-**dahl**-yah), medal, 18

la medicina (lah may-dee-**chee**-nah), medicine, 11

dal medico (dahl **may**-dee-koh), doctor's office, 11

medio (**may**-dee-oh), medium, 26

la medusa (lah may-**doo**-sah), jellyfish, 22

la mela (lah **may**-lah), apple, 6

la mela caramellata (lah **may**-lah kah-rah-mayl-**lah**-tah), caramel apple, 21

il melone (eel may-**loh**-nay), melon, 6

il menestrello (eel may-nay-**stray**l-loh), minstrel, 25

il mento (eel **mayn**-toh), chin, 11

il menù (eel may-**noo**), menu, 10

la merce imbarcata (lah **mayr**-chay eem-bahr-**kah**-tah), cargo bay, 23

metà (may-**tah**), half, 31

il meteorologo (eel may-tay-oh-**roh**-loh-goh), weather forecaster, 15

il metro a nastro (eel **may**-troh ah **nah**-stroh), tape measure, 3

il microfono (eel mee-**kroh**-foh-noh), microphone, 19

il microscopio (eel mee-kroh-**skoh**-pee-oh), microscope, 23

miliardo (meel-**yahr**-doh), billion, 31

milione (meel-**yoh**-nay), million, 31

mille (**meel**-lay), one thousand, 31

il miscelatore (eel mee-shay-lah-**toh**-ray), electric mixer, 3

il missile (eel **mees**-see-lay), rocket, 23

il molo (eel **moh**-loh), dock, 16

la moneta (lah moh-**nay**-tah), coin, 13

il monopattino (eel moh-noh-paht-**tee**-noh), scooter, 16

la montagna (lah mohn-**tah**-nyah), mountains, 32

morbido (**mohr**-bee-doh), soft, 26

la mosca (lah **moh**-skah), fly, 5

la mostarda (lah moh-**stahr**-dah), mustard, 10

la mostra dei talenti (lah **moh**-strah **day**-ee tah-**layn**-tee), talent show, 19

mostrare (moh-**strah**-ray), point (at), 27

la motocicletta (lah moh-toh-chee-**klayt**-tah), motorcycle, 16

il motore (eel moh-**toh**-ray), engine, 14, 17

il motoscafo (eel moh-toh-**skah**-foh), motorboat, 16

il mousse (eel moos), mousse, 12

la mucca (lah **mook**-kah), cow, 9

il museo (eel moo-**zay**-oh), museum, 8

la muta (lah **moo**-tah), wet suit, 22

il naso (eel **nah**-zo), nose, 11

il nastro d'imballaggio (eel **nah**-stroh deem-bahl-**lahj**-joh), packing tape, 13

la nave (lah **nah**-vay), cruise ship, 16

la navicella spaziale (lah nah-vee-**chayl**-lah spah-tsee-**ah**-lay), space shuttle, 23

il navigatore (eel nah-vee-gah-**toh**-ray), navigator, 17

la nebbia (lah **nayb**-bee-ah), fog, 5

la nebulosa (lah nay-boo-**loh**-zah), nebula, 23

il negozio dei gioccattoli (eel nay-**goh**-tsee-oh day-ee joh-**kaht**-toh-lee), toy store, 8

il negozio di confezioni (eel nay-**goh**-tsee-oh dee kohn-fay-tsee- **oh**-nee), clothing store, 8

neri (**nay**-ree), black, 12

nero (**nay**-roh), black, 28

la neve (lah **nay**-vay), snow, 5

il nido (eel **nee**-doh), bird's nest, 5

le noci (lay **noh**-chee), nuts, 6

il nodo (eel **noh**-doh), knot, 13

non tagliente (nohn tahl-**yayn**-tay), dull, 26

la nonna (lah **nohn**-nah), grandma, grandmother, 29

il nonno (eel **nohn**-noh), grandfather, grandpa, 29

nono (**noh**-noh), ninth, 31

nord (nohrd), north, 32

nord-est (nohrd-**ayst**), northeast, 32

nord-ovest (nohrd-oh-**vayst**), northwest, 32

la notte (lah **noht**-tay), night, 21

novanta (noh-**vahn**-tah), ninety, 31

novantacinque (noh-vahn-tah-**cheen**-kway), ninety-five, 31

novantadue (noh-vahn-tah-**doo**-ay), ninety-two, 31

novantanove (noh-vahn-tah-**noh**-vay), ninety-nine, 31

novantaquattro (noh-vahn-tah-**kwaht**-troh), ninety-four, 31

novantasei (noh-vahn-tah-**say**-ee), ninety-six, 31

novantasette (noh-vahn-tah-**sayt**-tay), ninety-seven, 31

novantatrè (noh-vahn-tah-**tray**), ninety-three, 31

novantotto (noh-vahn-**toht**-toh), ninety-eight, 31

novantuno (noh-vahn-**too**-noh), ninety-one, 31

nove (**noh**-vay), nine, 31

i numeri (ee **noo**-may-ree), numbers, 1, 31

i numeri cardinali (ee **noo**-may-ree kahr-dee-**nah**-lee), cardinal numbers, 31

i numeri ordinali (ee **noo**-may-ree ohr-dee-**nah**-lee), ordinal numbers, 31

nuotare (noo-oh-**tah**-ray), swim, 27

il nuoto (eel noo-**oh**-toh), swimming, 18

nuovo (noo-**oh**-voh), new, 26

le nuvole (lay **noo**-voh-lay), clouds, 5

l'oasi (**loh**-ah-zee), oasis, 32

l'oblò (**loh**-bloh), porthole, 22

l'oca (**loh**-kah), goose, 9

gli occhi (lyee **oh**-kee), eyes, 11

gli occhiali (lyee oh-kee-**ah**-lee), glasses, 7

gli occhiali di protezione (lyee oh-kee-**ah**-lee dee proh-tay-tsee- **oh**-nay), goggles, 18

gli occhiali scuri (lyee oh-kee-**ah**-lee **skoo**-ree), sunglasses, 7

l'oceano (loh-chay-**ah**-noh), ocean, 22

l'Oceano Artico (loh-chay-**ah**-noh **ahr**-tee-koh), Arctic Ocean, 32

l'Oceano Atlantico (loh-chay-**ah**-noh aht-**lahn**-tee-koh), Atlantic Ocean, 32

l'Oceano Indiano (loh-chay-**ah**-noh een-dee-**ah**-noh), Indian Ocean, 32

l'Oceano Pacifico (loh-chay-**ah**-noh pah-**chee**-fee-koh), Pacific Ocean, 32

l'olio (**loh**-lee-oh), oil, 14

l'ombra (**lohm**-brah), shadow, 9

l'ombrello (lohm-**brayl**-loh), umbrella, 4, 7

l'onda (**lohn**-dah), wave, 22

ondulati (ohn-doo-**lah**-tee), wavy, 12

l'operaia (loh-pay-**righ**-ah), factory worker, 15

l'orchestra (lohr-**kay**-strah), orchestra, 19

l'orecchino (loh-ray-**kee**-noh), earring, 7

l'orecchio (loh-**ray**-kee-oh), ear, 11

l'orma (**lohr**-mah), footprint, 23

l'oro (**loh**-roh), gold, 22

l'orologio (loh-roh-**loh**-joh), clock, 1; watch, 7

l'orsacchiotto (lohr-sah-kee-**oht**-toh), bear cub, 20; teddy bear, 4

l'orso (**lohr**-soh), bear, 20

l'orso bianco (**lohr**-soh bee-**ahn**-koh), polar bear, 20

l'orso panda (**lohr**-soh **pahn**-dah), panda, 20

gli ortaggi (lyee ohr-**tahj**-jee), vegetables, 6

l'orto (**lohr**-toh), vegetable garden, 5

l'ospedale (loh-spay-**dah**-lay), hospital, 8

l'osso (**lohs**-soh), bone, 24

l'ostrica (**loh**-stree-kah), clam, 22

l'ottagono (loht-**tah**-goh-noh), octagon, 30

ottanta (oht-**tahn**-tah), eighty, 31

ottantacinque (oht-tahn-tah-**cheen**-kway), eighty-five, 31

ottantadue (oht-tahn-tah-**doo**-ay), eighty-two, 31

ottantanove (oht-tahn-tah-**noh**-vay), eighty-nine, 31

ottantaquattro (oht-tahn-tah-**kwaht**-troh), eighty-four, 31

ottantasei (oht-tahn-tah-**say**-ee), eighty-six, 31

ottantasette (oht-tahn-tah-**sayt**-tay), eighty-seven, 31

ottantatrè (oht-tahn-tah-**tray**), eighty-three, 31

ottantotto (oht-tahn-**toht**-toh), eighty-eight, 31

ottantuno (oht-tahn-**too**-noh), eighty-one, 31

ottavo (oht-**tah**-voh), eighth, 31

l'ottico (**loht**-tee-koh), optician, 15

otto (**oht**-toh), eight, 31

l'ovale (loh-**vah**-lay), oval, 30

ovest (oh-**vayst**), west, 32

il pacco (eel **pahk**-koh), package, 13

il pacco per la spesa (eel **pahk**-koh payr lah **spay**-zah), shopping bag, 6

la padella (lah pah-**dayl**-lah), pan, 3

il padre (eel **pah**-dray), father, 29

il paese (eel pah-**ay**-say), country, 9

il pagliaccio (eel pahl-**yah**-choh), clown, 21

la pala (lah **pah**-lah), shovel, 5

il palcoscenico (eel pahl-koh-**shay**-nee-koh), stage, 19

la paletta della spazzatura (lah pah-**layt**-tah **dayl**-lah spah-tsah-**too**-rah), dustpan, 3

la palla (lah **pahl**-lah), baseball, football, soccer ball, 18

la pallacanestro (lah pahl-lah-kah-**nay**-stroh), basketball, 18

la pallavolo (lah pahl-**lah**-voh-loh), volleyball, 18

le palline di marmo (lay pahl-**lee**-nay dee **mahr**-moh), marbles, 4

il pallone (eel pahl-**loh**-nay), balloon, 21; hot-air balloon, 16

la palotta di neve (lah pah-**loht**-tah dee **nay**-vay), snowball, 5

la panca (lah **pahn**-kah), bench, 8

il pane (eel **pah**-nay), bread, 6

la panetteria (lah pahn-ayt-tay-**ree**-ah), bakery, 8

la **panna** (lah **pahn**-nah), cream, 10

il **pannello di controllo** (eel pahn-**nayl**-loh dee kohn-**trohl**-loh), control panel, 23

il **pannello solare** (eel pahn-**nayl**-loh soh-**lah**-ray), solar panel, 23

il **panno** (eel **pahn**-noh), cloth, 24

i **pantaloni** (ee pahn-tah-**loh**-nee), pants, 7

i **pantaloni della tuta** (ee pahn-tah-**loh**-nee **dayl**-lah **too**-tah), sweatpants, 7

il **papero** (eel **pah**-pay-roh), gosling, 9

il **pappagallo** (eel pahp-pah-**gahl**-loh), parrot, 20

il **parabrezza** (eel pah-rah-**bray**-tsah), windshield, 14

il **paracadute** (eel pah-rah-kah-**doo**-tay), parachute, 18

il **paracadutismo** (eel pah-rah-kah-doo-**teez**-moh), skydiving, 18

il **paraorecchie** (eel pah-rah-oh-**ray**-kee-ay), earmuffs, 7

la **parata di circo** (lah pah-**rah**-tah dee **cheer**-koh), circus parade, 21

i **paraurti** (ee pahr-ah-**oor**-tee), fender, 14

il **parcheggio** (eel pahr-**kay**-joh), parking lot, 8

il **parchimetro** (eel pahr-kee-**may**-troh), parking meter, 8

il **parco** (eel **pahr**-koh), park, 8

il **parco giochi** (eel **pahr**-koh **joh**-kee), playground, 8

la **parete** (lah pah-**ray**-tay), wall, 2

parlare (pahr-**lah**-ray), talk, 27

la **parrucca** (lah pahr-**rook**-kah), wig, 19

la **parrucchiera** (lah pahr-roo-kee-**ay**-rah), hairstylist, 12

il **passaggio pedonale** (eel pahs-**sah**-joh pay-doh-**nah**-lay), crosswalk, 16

il **passaporto** (eel pahs-sah-**pohr**-toh), passport, 17

il **passeggero** (eel pahs-say-**jay**-roh), passenger, 17

il **passeggino** (eel pahs-say-**jee**-noh), stroller, 16

il **passeggio nello spazio** (eel pahs-**say**-joh **nayl**-loh **spah**-tsee-oh), space walk, 23

la **pasta** (lah **pah**-stah), noodles, 10

il **pastello** (eel pah-**stayl**-loh), crayon, 1

i **pasti** (ee **pah**-stee), meals, 10

le **patate** (lay pah-**tah**-tay), potatoes, 6

le **patatine** (lay pah-tah-**tee**-nay), potato chips

le **patatine fritte** (lay pah-tah-**tee**-nay **freet**-tay), french fries, 10

il **pattinaggio** (eel paht-tee-**nah**-joh), skating, 18

pattinare (paht-tee-**nah**-ray), skate, 27

i **pattini** (ee paht-**tee**-nee), skates, 18

i **pattini a rotelle** (ee paht-**tee**-nee ah roh-**tayl**-lay), roller skates, 16

il **pavimento** (eel pah-vee-**mayn**-toh), floor, 2

il **pavone** (eel pah-**voh**-nay), peacock, 20

il **paziente** (eel pah-tsee-**ayn**-tay), patient, 11

la **pecora** (lah **pay**-koh-rah), sheep, 9

il **pedale** (eel pay-**dah**-lay), pedal, 14

la **pedicure** (lah pay-dee-**koo**-ray), pedicurist, 12

la **pelliccia** (lah payl-**lee**-chah), fur, 24

la **pellicola** (lah payl-**lee**-koh-lah), film, 21

la **penisola** (lah pay-**nee**-zoh-lah), peninsula, 32

la **penna** (lah **payn**-nah), pen, 1

il **pennello** (eel payn-**nayl**-loh), paintbrush, 1

pensare (payn-**sah**-ray), think, 27

il **pepe** (eel **pay**-pay), pepper, 10

la **perforatrice per carta** (lah payr-foh-rah-**tree**-chay payr **kahr**-tah), hole punch, 1

le **persiane** (lay payr-zee-**ah**-nay), venetian blinds, 2

pesante (pay-**zahn**-tay), heavy, 26

la **pesca** (lah **pay**-skah), (sport) fishing, 24

la **pesca** (lah **pay**-skah), (fruit) peach, 6

il **pescatore** (eel pay-skah-**toh**-ray), fisherman, 15

il **pesce** (eel **pay**-shay), fish, 1, 10

il **pesce angelo** (eel **pay**-shay ahn-**jay**-loh), angelfish, 22

il **pesce spada** (eel **pay**-shay **spah**-dah), swordfish, 22

il **petalo** (eel **pay**-tah-loh), petal, 5

il **pettine** (eel **payt**-tee-nay), comb, 12

il **petto** (eel **payt**-toh), chest, 11

il **pianeta** (eel pee-ah-**nay**-tah), planet, 23

piangere (pee-**ahn**-jay-ray), cry, 27

il **pianoforte** (eel pee-ah-noh-**fohr**-tay), piano, 19

la **pianta** (lah pee-**ahn**-tah), plant, 1

la **pianura** (lah pee-ah-**noo**-rah), plain, 32

i **piatti** (ee pee-**ah**-tee), cymbals, 19; dishes, 3

il **piattino** (eel pee-aht-**tee**-noh), saucer, 10

il **piatto** (eel pee-**aht**-toh), plate, 10

la **piazza** (lah pee-**ah**-tsah), square, 8

il **piccino** (eel pee-**chee**-noh), baby, 9

i **piccoli soldati** (ee **peek**-koh-lee sohl-**dah**-tee), toy soldiers, 4

piccolo (**peek**-koh-loh), small, 26

il **picnic** (eel **peek**-neek), picnic, 9

il **piede** (eel pee-**ay**-day), foot, 11

pieno (pee-**ay**-noh), full, 26

la **pigiama** (lah pee-**jah**-mah), pajamas, 7

la **pillola** (lah **peel**-loh-lah), pill, 11

il **pilota** (eel pee-**loh**-tah), pilot, 17

il **ping-pong** (eel **peeng**-pohng), table tennis, 18

il **pinguino** (eel peen-goo-ee-**ee**-noh), penguin, 20

la **pinna** (lah **peen**-nah), fin, 22; flipper, 22

la **pinza** (lah **peen**-tsah), pliers, 14

la **pioggia** (lah pee-**ohj**-jah), rain, 5

la **pioggia dei meteori** (lah pee-**ohj**-jah **day**-ee may-**tay**-oh-ree), meteor shower, 23

il **pipistrello** (eel pee-pee-**strayl**-loh), bat, 25

la **piscina** (lah pee-**shee**-nah), swimming pool, 18

i **piselli** (ee pee-**sayl**-lee), peas, 6

la **pista** (lah **pee**-stah), runway, 17

il **pittore** (eel peet-**toh**-ray), painter, 15

la **piuma** (lah pee-**oo**-mah), feather, 4

le **piume** (lay pee-**oo**-may), feathers, 20

il **poliziotto** (eel poh-lee-tsee-**oht**-toh), policeman, 15

il **pollice** (eel **pohl**-lee-chay), thumb, 11

il **pollo** (eel **pohl**-loh), chicken, 10

il **polo Nord** (eel **poh**-loh nohrd), North Pole, 32

il **polo Sud** (eel **poh**-loh sood), South Pole, 32

il **polpo** (eel **pohl**-poh), octopus, 22

la **poltrona** (lah pohl-**troh**-nah), armchair, 2

il **polvere** (eel **pohl**-vay-ray), dust, 4

i **pomodori** (ee poh-moh-**doh**-ree), tomatoes, 6

la **pompa della benzina** (lah **pohm**-pah **dayl**-lah bayn-**tsee**-nah), gas pump, 14

il **pompelmo** (eel pohm-**payl**-moh), grapefruit, 6

il **pompiere** (eel pohm-pee-**ay**-ray), fire fighter, 15

il **ponte** (eel **pohn**-tay), bridge, 16

il **ponte levatoio** (eel **pohn**-tay lay-vah-**toy**-oh), drawbridge, 25

il **popcorn** (eel **pohp**-kohrn), popcorn, 21

il **porcellino** (eel pohr-chayl-**lee**-noh), piglet, 9

la **porta** (lah **pohr**-tah), door, 2; gate, 17

il **portabagagli** (eel pohr-tah-bah-**gahl**-yee), trunk, 14

il **portabaglio** (eel pohr-tah-bah-**gahl**-yo), baggage handler, 17

il **portafoglio** (eel pohr-tah-**fohl**-yoh), wallet, 13

portare (pohr-**tah**-ray), carry, 27

il **portiere** (eel pohr-tee-**ay**-ray), doorman, 15

il **posapiedi** (eel poh-zah-pee-**ay**-dee), footstool, 2

il **postino** (eel poh-**stee**-noh), letter carrier, 15

il **posto di polizia** (eel **poh**-stoh dee poh-lee-**tsee**-ah), police station, 8

la **pozzanghera** (lah poh-**tsahn**-gay-rah), puddle, 5

il **pozzo** (eel **poh**-tsoh), well, 24

il **pranzo** (eel **prahn**-tsoh), lunch, 10

il **pranzo surgelato** (eel **prahn**-tsoh soor-jay-**lah**-toh), frozen dinner, 6

prendere (**prayn**-day-ray), catch, 27

i **preposizioni** (ee pray-poh-zee-tsee-**oh**-nee), prepositions, 26

la **presa** (lah **pray**-tsah), electrical outlet, 3

il **presentatore** (eel pray-zayn-tah-**toh**-ray), ringmaster, 21

il **prezzo** (eel **pray**-tsoh), price, 6

la **primavera** (lah pree-mah-**vay**-rah), spring, 5

primo (**pree**-moh), first, 31

il **principe** (eel **preen**-chee-pay), prince, 25

la **principessa** (la preen-chee-**pays**-sah), princess, 25

il **problema d'aritmetica** (eel proh-**blay**-mah dah-reet-**may**-tee-kah), arithmetic problem, 1

la **proboscide** (lah proh-boh-**shee**-day), trunk, 24

il **programmatore** (eel proh-grahm-mah-**toh**-ray), computer programmer, 15

il **proiettore** (eel proy-ayt-**toh**-ray), movie projector, 4

il **prontosoccorso** (eel **prohn**-toh sohk-**kohr**-soh), ambulance, 16

il **prosciutto** (eel proh-**shoot**-toh), ham, 10

la **provetta** (lah proh-**vayt**-tah), test tube, 23

il **pterodattilo** (eel tay-roh-**daht**-tee-loh), pterodactyl, 24

il **pubblico** (eel **poob**-blee-koh), audience, 19

il **pugilato** (eel poo-jee-**lah**-toh), boxing, 18

il **pulcino** (eel pool-**chee**-noh), chick, 9

il **puledro** (eel poo-**lay**-droh), colt, 9

pulito (poo-**lee**-toh), clean, 26

la **punta di freccia** (lah **poon**-tah dee **fray**-chah), arrowhead, 24

il **quaderno** (eel kwah-**dayr**-noh), notebook, 1

il **quadrato** (eel kwah-**drah**-toh), square, 30

il **quadro** (eel **kwah**-droh), picture, 1

quaranta (kwah-**rahn**-tah), forty, 31

quarantacinque (kwah-rahn-tah-**cheen**-kway), forty-five, 31

quarantadue (kwah-rahn-tah-**doo**-ay), forty-two, 31

quarantanove (kwah-rahn-tah-**noh**-vay), forty-nine, 31

quarantaquattro (kwah-rahn-tah-**kwaht**-troh), forty-four, 31

quarantasei (kwah-rahn-tah-**say**-ee), forty-six, 31

quarantasette (kwah-rahn-tah-**sayt**-tay), forty-seven, 31

quarantatrè (kwah-rahn-tah-**tray**), forty-three, 31

quarantotto (kwah-rahn-**toht**-toh), forty-eight, 31

quarantuno (kwah-rahn-**too**-noh), forty-one, 31

quarto (**kwahr**-toh), fourth, 31

quattordici (kwaht-**tohr**-dee-chee), fourteen, 31

quattro (**kwaht**-troh), four, 5, 31

quindici (**kween**-dee-chee), fifteen, 31

quinto (**kween**-toh), fifth, 31

la **racchetta** (lah rahk-**kayt**-tah), racket, 18; tennis racket, 17

la **raccolta** (lah rahk-**kohl**-tah), crop, 24

la radio (lah **rah**-dee-oh), radio, 2
la ragazza (lah rah-**gah**-tsah), girl, 9
i ragazzi (ee rah-**gah**-tsee), children, 19
il ragazzo (eel rah-**gah**-tsoh), boy, 9
i raggi (ee **rahj**-jee), spokes, 14
i raggi X (ee **rahj**-jee eeks), X ray, 11
la ragnatela (lah rah-nyah-**tay**-lah), cobweb, 4; spiderweb, 25
il ragno (eel **rah**-nyoh), spider, 25
il ramo (eel **rah**-moh), branch, 5
la rana (lah **rah**-nah), frog, 9
rapido (**rah**-pee-doh), fast, 26
il rasoio (eel rah-**zoy**-oh), razor, 12
il rastrello (eel rah-**strayl**-loh), rake, 5
il ratto (eel **raht**-tsah), rat, 25
la razza (lah **rah**-tsah), stingray, 22
il re (eel ray), king, 25
il recinto (eel ray-**cheen**-toh), fence, 9
il recinto con sabbia (eel ray-**cheen**-toh kohn **sahb**-bee-ah), sandbox, 8
il regalo (eel ray-**gah**-loh), gift, 10
la regina (lah ray-**jee**-nah), queen, 25
la regola (lah **ray**-goh-lah), ruler, 1
il relitto di nave naufragio (eel ray-**leet**-toh dee **nah**-vay now-**frah**-joh), shipwreck, 22
il remo (eel **ray**-moh), oar, 16
la rete (lah **ray**-tay), net, 18
la rete di sicurezza (lah **ray**-tay dee see-koo-**ray**-tsah), safety net, 21
il rettangolo (eel rayt-**tahn**-goh-loh), rectangle, 30
il revelatore del metallo (eel ray-vay-lah-**toh**-ray dayl may-**tahl**-loh), metal detector, 17
ricci (**ree**-chee), curly, 12
il riccio di mare (eel **ree**-choh dee **mah**-ray), sea urchin, 22
ricevere (ree-**chay**-vay-ray), receive, 27
ridere (**ree**-day-ray), laugh, 27
il riflettore (eel ree-flay-**toh**-ray), flashbulb, 21
i riflettori (ee ree-flayt-**toh**-ree), reflectors, 14
il rimorchiatore (eel ree-mohr-kee-ah-**toh**-ray), tugboat, 16
il rinoceronte (eel ree-noh-chay-**rohn**-tay), rhinoceros, 20
il riso (eel **ree**-zoh), rice, 10
il ristorante (eel ree-stoh-**rahn**-tay), restaurant, 8, 10
il ritiro bagagli (eel ree-**tee**-roh bah-**gahl**-yee), baggage claim, 17
le riviste (lay ree-**vee**-stay), magazines, 11
il robot (eel **roh**-boht), robot, 23
la roccia (lah **roh**-chah), rock, 24
rompere (**rohm**-pay-ray), break, 27
il rompicapo (eel rohm-pee-**kah**-poh), jigsaw puzzle, 4
rosa (**roh**-zah), pink, 28
il rossetto (eel rohs-**sayt**-toh), lipstick, 12
rossi (**rohs**-see), red, 12
rosso (**rohs**-soh), red, 28
il rosso d'uovo (eel **rohs**-soh doo-**oh**-voh), yolk, 10
le rotaie (lay roh-**tigh**-ay), train tracks, 9
il rubinetto (eel roo-bee-**nayt**-toh), faucet, 3
ruggire (roo-**jee**-ray), roar, 27
la ruota (lah roo-**oh**-tah), wheel, 24
la ruota di carretta (lah roo-**oh**-tah dee kahr-**rayt**-tah), cartwheel, 21
le ruote speciali (lay roo-**oh**-tay spay-**chah**-lee), training wheels, 14

la sabbia (lah **sahb**-bee-ah), sand, 22
il sacco a pelo (eel **sahk**-koh ah **pay**-loh), sleeping bag, 9

il sacco da posta (eel **sahk**-koh da **poh**-stah), mailbag, 13
il sacco per abiti (eel **sahk**-koh payr **ah**-bee-tee), garment bag, 17
la sala da pranzo (lah **sah**-lah dah **prahn**-zoh), dining room, 2
il sale (eel **sah**-lay), salt, 10
salire (sah-**lee**-ray), climb, 27
il salotto (eel sah-**loht**-toh), living room, 2
le salsicce (lay sahl-**see**-chay), sausages, 10
saltare (sahl-**tah**-ray), jump, 27
il salto in alto (eel **sahl**-toh een **ahl**-toh), high jump, 18
il salto in lungo (eel **sahl**-toh een **loon**-goh), long jump, 18
il salto mortale (eel **sahl**-toh mohr-**tah**-lay), somersault, 21
il salvadanaio (eel sahl-vah-dah-**nigh**-oh), piggy bank, 13
i sandali (ee **sahn**-dah-lee), sandals, 7
il sangue (eel **sahn**-gway), blood, 11
il sapone (eel sah-**poh**-nay), soap, 6
il saracco (eel sah-**rahk**-koh), saw, 3
il sarto (eel **sahr**-toh), tailor, 15
il sassofono (eel sahs-**soh**-foh-noh), saxophone, 19
il satellite (eel sah-tayl-**lee**-tay), satellite, 23
lo scaffale (loh skahf-**fah**-lay), bookcase, 1; shelf, 2
le scaglie (lay **skahl**-yay), scales, 22
la scala a pioli (lah **skah**-lah ah pee-**oh**-lee), ladder, 23
la scala di sicurezza (lah **skah**-lah dee see-koo-**ray**-tsah), fire escape, 8
la scala mobile (lah **skah**-lah **moh**-bee-lay), escalator, 17
la scala per arrampicarsi (lah **skah**-lah payr ahr-rahm-pee-**kahr**-see), rope ladder, 21
le scale (lay **skah**-lay), stairs, 2
le scarpe (lay **skahr**-pay), shoes, 7
le scarpe da tennis (lay skahr-**pay** dah **tayn**-nees), gym shoes, 7
le scarpette da ballo (lay skahr-**payt**-tay dah **bahl**-loh), ballet slippers, 19
gli scarponi (lyee skahr-**poh**-nee), hiking boots, 7
la scatola (lah **skah**-toh-lah), box, 4; can, 6
la scatola degli utensili (lah **skah**-toh-lah **dayl**-yee oo-**tayn**-zee-lee), toolbox, 3
la scatola della musica (lah **skah**-toh-lah **dayl**-lah **moo**-zee-kah), music box, 4
scavare (skah-**vah**-ray), dig, 27
il scenario (eel shay-**nahr**-ee-oh), scenery, 19
lo schedario (loh skay-**dah**-ree-oh), file cabinet, 13
lo scheletro (loh skay-**lay**-troh), skeleton, 24
lo schermo di radar (loh **skayr**-moh dee **rah**-dahr), radar screen, 17
la schiena (lah skee-**ay**-nah), back, 11
la schiuma di sapone (lah **skyoo**-mah dee sah-**poh**-nay), suds, 12
gli sci (lyee shee), skis, 18
lo sci alpino (loh shee ahl-**pee**-noh), downhill skiing, 18
sciare (**shah**-ray), ski, 27
la sciarpa (lah **shahr**-pah), scarf, 7
lo scienziato (loh shayn-zee-**ah**-toh), scientist, 23
la scimmia (lah **sheem**-mee-ah), monkey, 20
la scivola (lah **shee**-voh-lah), slide, 8
la scodella (lah skoh-**dayl**-lah), bowl, 10
la scopa (lah **skoh**-pah), broom, 3
la scopa di stracci (lah **skoh**-pah dee **strah**-chee), mop, 3

la scriminatura (lah skree-mee-nah-**too**-rah), part, 12
scrivere (**skree**-vay-ray), write, 27
lo scudiero (loh skoo-dee-**ay**-roh), squire, 25
lo scudo (loh **skoo**-doh), shield, 25
la scuola (lah skoo-**oh**-lah), school, 8
scuro (**skoo**-roh), dark, 26
la secchia (lah **say**-kee-ah), bucket, 24
secco (**say**-koh), dry, 26
la seconda pilota (lah say-**kohn**-dah pee-**loh**-tah), copilot, 17
secondo (say-**kohn**-doh), second, 31
il sedano (eel **say**-dah-noh), celery, 10
sedersi (say-**dayr**-see), sit down, 27
la sedia (lah **say**-dee-ah), chair, 3
la sedia a dondolo (lah **say**-dee-ah ah **dohn**-doh-loh), rocking chair, 2, 4
la sedia a rotelle (lah **say**-dee-ah ah roh-**tayl**-lay), wheelchair, 11
sedici (**say**-dee-chee), sixteen, 31
il sedile (eel say-**dee**-lay), seat, 17
il sedile del guidatore (eel say-**dee**-lay dayl gwee-dah-**toh**-ray), driver's seat, 14
il sedile del passeggero (eel say-**dee**-lay dayl pahs-sayj-**jay**-roh), passenger's seat, 14
il sedile posteriore (eel say-**dee**-lay poh-stay-ree-**oh**-ray), backseat, 14
il segnale (eel say-**nyah**-lay), sign, 8
la segretaria (lah say-gray-tah-**ree**-ah), receptionist, 13; secretary, 15
sei (**say**-ee), six, 31
la selce (lah **sayl**-chay), flint, 24
la sella (lah **sayl**-lah), saddle, 25
il semaforo (eel say-**mah**-foh-roh), traffic lights, 8, 16
il serpente (eel sayr-**payn**-tay), snake, 20
la serratura (lah sayr-rah-**too**-rah), lock, 13
il servizio per le automobili (eel sayr-**vee**-tsee-oh payr lay ow- toh-**moh**-bee-lee), drive-in, 13
sessanta (says-**sahn**-tah), sixty, 31
sessantacinque (says-sahn-tah-**cheen**-kway), sixty-five, 31
sessantadue (says-sahn-tah-**doo**-ay), sixty-two, 31
sessantanove (says-sahn-tah-**noh**-vay), sixty-nine, 31
sessantaquattro (says-sahn-tah-**kwaht**-troh), sixty-four, 31
sessantasei (says-sahn-tah-**say**-ee), sixty-six, 31
sessantasette (says-sahn-tah-**sayt**-tay), sixty-seven, 31
sessantatrè (says-sahn-tah-**tray**), sixty-three, 31
sessantotto (says-sahn-**toht**-toh), sixty-eight, 31
sessantuno (says-sahn-**too**-noh), sixty-one, 31
sesto (**say**-stoh), sixth, 31
settanta (sayt-**tahn**-tah), seventy, 31
settantacinque (sayt-tahn-tah-**cheen**-kway), seventy-five, 31
settantadue (sayt-tahn-tah-**doo**-ay), seventy-two, 31
settantanove (sayt-tahn-tah-**noh**-vay), seventy-nine, 31
settantaquattro (sayt-tahn-tah-**kwaht**-troh), seventy-four, 31
settantasei (sayt-tahn-tah-**say**-ee), seventy-six, 31
settantasette (sayt-tahn-tah-**sayt**-tay), seventy-seven, 31
settantatrè (sayt-tahn-tah-**tray**), seventy-three, 31
settantotto (sayt-tahn-**toht**-toh), seventy-eight, 31
settantuno (sayt-tahn-**too**-noh), seventy-one, 31
sette (**sayt**-tay), seven, 31
settimo (**sayt**-tee-moh), seventh, 31

lo **shampoo** (loh shahm-**poo**), shampoo, 12
il **silofono** (eel see-**loh**-foh-noh), xylophone, 19
sinistro (see-**nee**-stroh), left, 26
il **sipario** (eel see-**pah**-ree-oh), curtain, 19
il **sistema solare** (eel see-**stay**-mah soh-**lah**-ray), solar system, 23
lo **skateboard** (loh skateboard), skateboard, 16
la **slitta** (lah **sleet**-tah), sled, 5
lo **smalto** (loh **smahl**-toh), nail polish, 12
la **soffitta** (lah sohf-**feet**-tah), attic, 4
il **soffitto** (eel sohf-**feet**-toh), ceiling, 2
il **sole** (eel **soh**-lay), sun, 23
il **sollevamento di pesi** (eel sohl-lay-vah-**mayn**-toh dee **pay**-zee), weight lifting, 18
il **sommergibile** (eel sohm-mayr-**jee**-bee-lay), submarine, 22
sopra (**soh**-prah), above, 26
il **sopracciglio** (eel soh-prah-**cheel**-yoh), eyebrow, 11
la **sorella** (lah soh-**rayl**-lah), sister, 29
il **sorriso** (eel sohr-**ree**-zoh), smile, 11
sotto (soht-**toh**), under, 26
la **spada** (lah **spah**-dah), sword, 25
lo **spago** (loh **spah**-goh), string, 4, 13
la **spalla** (lah **spahl**-lah), shoulder, 11
la **spatola** (lah **spah**-toh-lah), spatula, 3
lo **spazio** (loh **spah**-tsee-oh), space, 23
lo **spazzaneve** (loh spah-tsah-**nay**-vay), snowplow, 5
la **spazzatura** (lah spah-tsah-**too**-rah), trash, 1
la **spazzola** (lah spah-**tsoh**-lah), brush, 12
lo **spazzolino da denti** (loh spah-tsoh-**lee**-noh dah **dayn**-tee), toothbrush, 11
lo **specchietto retrovisore** (loh spayk-kee-**ayt**-toh ray-troh-vee-zoh-ray), rearview mirror, 14
lo **specchio** (loh **spayk**-kee-oh), mirror, 2
spento (**spayn**-toh), off, 26
la **spiaggia** (lah spee-**ahj**-jah), beach, 8
gli **spinaci** (lyee spee-**nah**-chee), spinach, 6
spingere (**speen**-jay-ray), push, 27
sporco (**spohr**-koh), dirty, 26
sport (sport), sports, 18
lo **sportello bagagli** (loh spohr-**tayl**-loh bah-**gahl**-yee), baggage check-in, 17
lo **sportello dei biglietti** (loh spohr-**tayl**-loh day-ee beel-**yayt**-tee), ticket counter, 17
lo **spruzzatore** (lo sproo-tsah-**toh**-ray), sprinkler, 5
lo **spruzzo** (loh **sproo**-tsoh), hair spray, 12
la **spugna** (lah **spoo**-nyah), sponge, 3
lo **squalo** (loh **skwah**-loh), shark, 22
la **staffa** (lah **stahf**-fah), stirrup, 25
le **stagioni** (lay stah-**joh**-nee), seasons, 5
lo **stagno** (loh **stah**-nyoh), pond, 9
la **stalla** (lah **stahl**-lah), stable, 25
la **stanza da bagno** (lah **stahn**-zah dah **bah**-nyoh), bathroom, 2
lo **starnuto** (loh stahr-**noo**-toh), sneeze, 11
la **statua** (lah **stah**-too-ah), statue, 8
la **stazione** (lah stah-tsee-**oh**-nay), train station, 8
la **stazione dei pompieri** (lah stah-tsee-**oh**-nay day-ee pohm-pee-**ay**-ree), fire station, 8
la **stazione di servizio** (lah stah-tsee-**oh**-nay dee sayr-**vee**-tsee-oh), gas station, 14
la **stazione spaziale** (lah stah-tsee-**oh**-nay spah-tsee-**ah**-lay), space station, 23
la **stella di mare** (lah **stayl**-lah dee **mah**-ray), starfish, 22
le **stelle** (lay **stayl**-lay), stars, 23
lo **stelo** (loh **stay**-loh), stem, 5
lo **stendardo** (loh stayn-**dahr**-doh), banner, 25

lo **stetoscopio** (loh stay-toh-**skoh**-pee-oh), stethoscope, 11
la **stilista** (lah stee-**lee**-stah), fashion designer, 15
gli **stivali** (lyee stee-**vah**-lee), boots, 7
gli **stivali di cowboy** (lyee stee-**vah**-lee dee **kow**-boy), cowboy boots, 4
stop (stohp), stop!, 16
lo **stop** (loh stohp), stop sign, 16
la **storia** (lah **stoh**-ree-ah), history, 24
la **storia umana** (lah **stoh**-ree-ah oo-**mah**-nah), human history, 24
la **strada** (lah **strah**-dah), road, 9; street, 16
la **strada privata** (lah **strah**-dah pree-**vah**-tah), driveway, 8
stretto (**strayt**-toh), narrow, 26
la **stringa** (lah **streen**-gah), shoelace, 7
le **striscie** (lay **stree**-shay), stripes, 20
lo **struzzo** (loh **stroo**-tsoh), ostrich, 20
il **su in giù** (eel soo een joo), seesaw, 8
su (soo), on top of, 26
il **succo** (eel **sook**-koh), fruit juice, 6
sud (sood), south, 32
sud-est (sood-**ayst**), southeast, 32
sud-ovest (sood-oh-**vayst**), southwest, 32
suonare (soo-oh-**nah**-ray), play (an instrument), 27
il **supermercato** (eel soo-payr-mayr-**kah**-toh), supermarket, 6
la **sveglia** (lah **zvayl**-yah), alarm clock, 2
la **svizzera** (lah **zvee**-tsay-rah), hamburger, 10

tagliare (tal-**yah**-ray), cut, 27
il **tagliaunghie** (eel tahl-yah-**oon**-gee-ay), nail clippers, 12
tagliente (tahl-yee-**ayn**-tay), sharp, 26
il **taglio a spazzola** (eel **tahl**-yoh ah **spah**-tsoh-lah), crew cut, 12
il **tamburo** (eel tahm-**boo**-roh), drum, 19
il **tampone** (eel tahm-**poh**-nay), ink pad, 13
il **tappeto** (eel tahp-**pay**-toh), rug, 1; carpet, 2
la **tartaruga** (lah tahr-tah-**roo**-gah), turtle, 20
la **tartaruga di mare** (lah tahr-tah-**roo**-gah dee **mah**-ray), sea turtle, 22
la **tasca** (lah **tah**-skah), pocket, 7
il **tassì** (eel tahs-**see**), taxi, 16
il **tassista** (eel tahs-**see**-stah), taxi driver, 15
la **tavola** (lah **tah**-voh-lah), board, 3; table, 3
la **tavola calda** (lah **tah**-voh-lah **kahl**-dah), snack bar, 17
la **tavola da esaminare** (lah **tah**-voh-lah dah ay-zah-mee-**nah**-ray), examining table, 11
la **tavola da stiro** (lah **tah**-voh-lah dah **stee**-roh), ironing board, 3
il **tavolo** (eel **tah**-voh-loh), night table, 2
la **tazza** (lah **tah**-tsah), cup, 10
il **tè** (eel tay), tea, 10
il **tecnico video** (eel **tayk**-nee-koh **vee**-day-oh), television repairer, 15
il **telaio** (eel tay-**ligh**-oh), loom, 24
la **telecamera di sicurezza** (lah tay-lay-**kah**-may-rah dee see-koo-**ray**-tsah), security camera, 13
il **telefono** (eel tay-**lay**-foh-noh), telephone, 2
il **televisore** (eel tay-lay-vee-**zoh**-ray), television, 2
il **temperamatite** (eel taym-payr-ah-mah-**tee**-tay), pencil sharpener, 1
il **tempo** (eel **taym**-poh), weather, 5
la **tenda** (lah **tayn**-dah), big top, 21; tent, 9
le **tendine** (lay **tayn**-dee-nay), curtains, 2

il **tennis** (eel **tay**-nees), tennis, 18
il **tentacolo** (eel tayn-**tah**-koh-loh), tentacle, 22
il **tergicristallo** (eel tayr-jee-kree-**stahl**-loh), windshield wipers, 14
il **termometro** (eel tayr-**moh**-may-troh), thermometer, 11
la **terra** (lah **tayr**-rah), dirt, 9
la **Terra** (lah **tayr**-rah), Earth, 23
terzo (**tayr**-tsoh), third, 31
il **tesoro** (eel tay-**zoh**-roh), treasure, 22
la **tessitrice** (lah tays-see-**tree**-chay), weaver, 24
la **testa** (lah **tays**-tah), head, 11
il **tettino** (eel tayt-**tee**-noh), sunroof, 14
il **tetto** (eel **tayt**-toh), roof, 2
il **tiglio** (eel **teel**-yoh), lime, 6
la **tigre** (lah **tee**-gray), tiger, 20
la **tigre preistorica** (lah **tee**-gray pray-ee-**stoh**-ree-kah), saber-toothed tiger, 24
il **tigrotto** (eel tee-**groht**-toh), tiger cub, 20
il **timbro** (eel **teem**-broh), rubber stamp, 13
il **timbro postale** (eel **teem**-broh poh-**stah**-lay), postmark, 13
tirare (tee-**rah**-ray), pull, 27
la **toletta** (lah toh-**layt**-tah), dresser, 2; toilet, 2
il **topo** (eel **toh**-poh), mouse, 9
il **toro** (eel **toh**-roh), bull, 9
la **torre** (lah **tohr**-ray), tower, 25
la **torre di controllo** (lah **tohr**-ray dee kohn-**trohl**-loh), control tower, 17
la **torta** (lah **tohr**-tah), cake, 10; pie, 6
il **tostatore** (eel toh-stah-**toh**-ray), toaster, 3
la **tovaglia** (lah toh-**vahl**-yah), tablecloth, 10
il **tovagliolo** (eel toh-vahl-**yoh**-loh), napkin, 10
tra (trah), between, 26
il **tramezzino** (eel trah-may-**tsee**-noh), sandwich, 10
i **trampoli** (ee trahm-**poh**-lee), stilts, 21
il **trapano** (eel **trah**-pah-noh), drill, 3
il **trapezio** (eel trah-**pay**-tsee-oh), trapeze, 21
il **trapezista** (eel trah-pay-**tsee**-stah), trapeze artist, 21
il **trasporto** (eel trahs-**pohr**-toh), transportation, 16
il **trattore** (eel traht-**toh**-ray), tractor, 9
tre (tray), three, 31
la **treccia** (lah **tray**-chah), braid, 12
tredici (**tray**-dee-chee), thirteen, 31
il **trenino** (eel tray-**nee**-noh), electric train, 4
il **treno** (eel **tray**-noh), train, 16
trenta (**trayn**-tah), thirty, 31
trentacinque (trayn-tah-**cheen**-kway), thirty-five, 31
trentadue (trayn-tah-**doo**-ay), thirty-two, 31
trentanove (trayn-tah-**noh**-vay), thirty-nine, 31
trentaquattro (trayn-tah-**kwaht**-troh), thirty-four, 31
trentasei (trayn-tah-**say**-ee), thirty-six, 31
trentasette (trayn-tah-**sayt**-tay), thirty-seven, 31
trentatrè (trayn-tah-**tray**), thirty-three, 31
trentotto (trayn-**toht**-toh), thirty-eight, 31
trentuno (trayn-**too**-noh), thirty-one, 31
il **triangolo** (eel tree-**ahn**-goh-loh), triangle, 30
il **tricheco** (eel tree-**kay**-koh), walrus, 20
il **triciclo** (eel tree-**chee**-kloh), tricycle, 14
il **trofeo** (eel troh-**fay**-oh), trophy, 18
la **tromba** (lah **trohm**-bah), trumpet, 19
il **trombone** (eel trohm-**boh**-nay), trombone, 19
il **trono** (eel **troh**-noh), throne, 25
trovare (troh-**vah**-ray), find, 27
il **trucco** (eel **trook**-koh), makeup, 19
la **tuba** (lah **too**-bah), tuba, 19
tuffare (toof-**fah**-ray), dive, 27

il tuffarsi (eel toof-**fahr**-see), diving, 18

il tuffatore subacqueo (eel toof-fah-**toh**-ray soo-bah-**kway**-oh), scuba diver, 22

la tundra (lah **toon**-drah), tundra, 32

il turbano (eel toor-**bah**-noh), turban, 21

il turbine di neve (eel toor-**bee**-nay dee **nay**-vay), snowstorm, 5

la tuta (lah **too**-tah), coveralls, 14

la tuta spaziale (lah **too**-tah spah-tsee-**ah**-lay), space suit, 23

il tutù (eel too-**too**), tutu, 19

l'uccello (loo-**chayl**-loh), bird, 5

l'ufficio postale (loof-**fee**-choh poh-**stah**-lay), post office, 13

umido (**oo**-mee-doh), wet, 26

undici (**oon**-dee-chee), eleven, 31

l'unghia (**loon**-gee-ah), fingernail, 12

l'unghia del piede (**loon**-gee-ah dayl pee-**ay**-day), toenail, 12

l'uniciclo (loon-ee-**chee**-kloh), unicycle, 21

l'unicorno (loon-ee-**kohr**-noh), unicorn, 25

uno (**oo**-noh), one, 31

l'uomo (loo-**oh**-moh), man, 9

l'uomo di neve (loo-**oh**-moh dee **nay**-vay), snowman, 5

le uova (lay oo-**oh**-vah), eggs, 6

le uva (lay **oo**-vah), grapes, 6

la valigia (lah vah-**lee**-jah), suitcase, 17

il vasaio (eel vah-**sigh**-oh), potter, 24

la vasca (lah **vah**-skah), bathtub, 2

il vaso (eel **vah**-zoh), pot, 24; vase, 2

il vassoio (eel vahs-**soy**-oh), tray, 10

vecchio (**vayk**-kee-oh), old, 26

la vela (lah **vay**-lah), sail, 16

vendere (**vayn**-day-ray), sell, 27

il venditore di libri (eel vayn-dee-**toh**-ray dee **lee**-bree), bookseller, 15

venire (vay-**nee**-ray), come, 27

il ventaglio (eel vayn-**tal**-yoh), fan, 4

venti (**vayn**-tee), twenty, 31

venticinque (vayn-tee-**cheen**-kway), twenty-five, 31

ventidue (vayn-tee-**doo**-ay), twenty-two, 31

il ventilatore (eel vayn-tee-lah-**toh**-ray), fan, 5

ventinove (vayn-tee-**noh**-vay), twenty-nine, 31

ventiquattro (vayn-tee-**kwaht**-troh), twenty-four, 31

ventisei (vayn-tee-**say**-ee), twenty-six, 31

ventisette (vayn-tee-**sayt**-tay), twenty-seven, 31

ventitrè (vayn-tee-**tray**), twenty-three, 31

il vento (eel **vayn**-toh), wind, 5

ventotto (vayn-**toht**-toh), twenty-eight, 31

ventuno (vayn-**too**-noh), twenty-one, 31

la veranda (lah vay-**rahn**-dah), deck, 5

verde (**vayr**-day), green, 28

il verme (eel **vayr**-may), worm, 5

la verticale (lah vayr-tee-**kah**-lay), handstand, 21

la verticale sulla testa (lah vayr-tee-**kah**-lay **sool**-lah **tay**-stah), headstand, 21

il veste da ballo (eel **vay**-stay dah **bahl**-loh), ball gown, 4

il vestito (eel vay-**stee**-toh), dress, 7

il veterinario (eel vay-tay-ree-**nah**-ree-oh), veterinarian, 15

vicino (vee-**chee**-noh), near, 26

vicino a (vee-**chee**-noh ah), next to, 26

il video camera (eel **vee**-day-oh **kah**-may-rah), video camera, 17

il videoregistratore (eel vee-day-oh-ray-jee-strah-**toh**-ray), videocassette player, 2

il villaggio (eel veel-**lah**-joh), village, 24

viola (vee-**oh**-lah), purple, 28

il violino (eel vee-oh-**lee**-noh), violin, 19

il violoncello (eel vee-oh-loh-**chayl**-loh), cello, 19

la vite (lah **vee**-tay), screw, 3

il vitello (eel vee-**tayl**-loh), calf, 9

il volano (eel voh-**lah**-noh), badminton, 18

il volante (eel voh-**lahn**-tay), steering wheel, 14

volare (voh-**lah**-ray), fly, 27

la volpe (lah **vohl**-pay), fox, 20

il vulcano (eel vool-**kah**-noh), volcano, 32

vuoto (voo-**oh**-toh), empty, 26

lo zaino (loh **tsigh**-noh), backpack, 7

la zampa (lah **tsahm**-pah), paw, 20

la zanna (lah **tsahn**-nah), tusk, 24

la zebra (lah **tsay**-brah), zebra, 20

lo zero (loh **tsay**-roh), zero, 31

la zia (lah **tsee**-ah), aunt, 29

lo zio (loh **tsee**-oh), uncle, 29

lo zoccolo (loh **tsohk**-koh-loh), hoof, 20

lo zoo (loh **tsoh**-oh), zoo, 20

lo zoologo (loh tsoh-**oh**-loh-goh), zookeeper, 20

lo zucchero (loh tsoo-**kay**-roh), sugar, 10

lo zucchero filato (loh tsoo-**kay**-roh fee-**lah**-toh), cotton candy, 21

lo zufolo (loh **tsoo**-foh-loh), whistle, 4

la zuppa (lah **tsoop**-pah), soup, 10

English-Italian Glossary and Index

cement mixer, la betoniera, 16
cereal, i cereali, 6
chain mail, la maglia di ferro, 25
chair, la sedia, 3
chalk, il gesso, 1
chalkboard, la lavagna, 1
channel, il canale, 32
check, l'assegno, 13
checkbook, il libretto d'assegni, 13
checkers, il gioco della dama, 4
cheek, la guancia, 11
cheese, il formaggio, 6
cherries, le ciliege, 6
chess, il gioco degli scacchi, 4
chest, il petto, 11
chick, il pulcino, 9
chicken, il pollo, 10
children, i ragazzi, 19
chimney, il camino, 2
chin, il mento, 11
chocolate, la cioccolata, 6
church, la chiesa, 8
circle, il circolo, 30
circus, il circo, 21
circus parade, la parata di circo, 21
city, la città, 8
clam, l'ostrica, 22
clarinet, il clarinetto, 19
classroom, la classe, 1
claws, l'artiglio, 20
clay, l'argilla, 24
clean, pulito, 26
climb, salire, 27
clock, l'orologio, 1
close, chiudere, 27
closed, chiuso, 26
closet, l'armadio a muro, 2
cloth, il panno, 24
clothes dryer, l'asciugatrice, 3
clothing, gli abiti, 7
clothing store, il negozio di confezioni, 8
clouds, le nuvole, 5
clown, il pagliaccio, 21
club, il bastone, 24
coat, il cappotto, 7
cobweb, la ragnatela, 4
coffee, il caffè, 10
coin, la moneta, 13
cold, freddo, 26
collar, il collo, 7
colored pencils, le matite colorate, 1
coloring book, il libro di disegni, 4
colors, colori, 28
colt, il puledro, 9
comb, il pettine, 12
come, venire, 27
comet, la cometa, 23
comic books, i giornali a fumetti, 4
community, la comunità, 15
compact disc, il compact disc, 2
compass (drawing), il compasso, 1; (magnetic), il compasso, 32
computer, il computer, 23
computer programmer, il programmatore, 15
Concorde, il Concorde, 17
conductor, il direttore d'orchestra, 19
cone, il cono, 30
constellation, la costellazione, 23
construction worker, il manovale, 15
control panel, il pannello di controllo, 23
control tower, la torre di controllo, 17
cook (verb), cucinare, 27; (noun), il cuoco, 15
cookies, i biscotti, 6
copilot, la seconda pilota, 17
coral, il corallo, 22
coral reef, il banco corallifero, 22
corn, il granturco, 24
corner, l'angolo, 8
costume, il costume, 19
cotton candy, lo zucchero filato, 21
counter, il banco, 3
country, il paese, 9
court jester, il burlone, 25

courtyard, il cortile, 25
cousin (female), la cugina, 29; (male), il cugino, 29
coveralls, la tuta, 14
cow, la mucca, 9
cowboy, il cowboy, 15
cowboy boots, gli stivali di cowboy, 4
cowboy hat, il cappello di cowboy, 4
crab, il granchio, 22
crackers, i crackers, 6
cradle, la culla, 4
crane, la gru, 8
crater, il cratere, 23
crayon, il pastello, 1
cream, la panna, 10
credit card, la carta di credito, 13
crew cut, il taglio a spazzola, 12
crop, la raccolta, 24
cross-country skiing, il fondo, 18
crosswalk, il passaggio pedonale, 16
crown, la corona, 25
cruise ship, la nave, 16
crutch, la gruccia, 11
cry, piangere, 27
cube, il cubo, 30
cup, la tazza, 10
curlers, i bigodini, 12
curling iron, il ferro per arricciare i capelli, 12
curly, ricci, 12
curtain (theater), il sipario, 19
curtains (home), le tendine, 2
customs officer, l'agente doganale, 17
cut, tagliare, 27
cycling, il ciclismo, 18
cylinder, il cilindro, 30
cymbals, i piatti, 19

dad, il babbo, 29
dance, ballare, 27
dancer, la ballerina, 19
dark, scuro, 26
dashboard, il cruscotto, 14
daughter, la figlia, 29
deck, la veranda, 5
deer, il cervo, 20
dental floss, la bavella, 11
dental hygienist, l'assistente del dentista, 11
dentist, il dentista, 11
dentist's office, dal dentista, 11
desert, il deserto, 32
desk (teacher's), la cattedra, 1; (pupil's), il banco, 1
dice, i dadi, 4
difficult, difficile, 26
dig, scavare, 27
dining room, la sala da pranzo, 2
dinner, la cena, 10
dinosaur, il dinosauro, 24
dirt, la terra, 9
dirty, sporco, 26
disc jockey, il disc jockey, 15
dishes, i piatti, 3
dishwasher, il lavapiatti, 3
dive, tuffare, 27
diving, il tuffarsi, 18
dock, il molo, 16
doctor, la dottoressa, 11
doctor's office, dal medico, 11
dog, il cane, 9
doll, la bambola, 4
dollhouse, la casa da bambole, 4
dolphin, il delfino, 22
donkey, l'asino, 9
door, la porta, 2
door handle, la maniglia, 14
doorman, il portiere, 15
down, in giù, 26
down vest, il gilè di piuma, 7
downhill skiing, lo sci alpino, 18
dragon, il drago, 25
draw, disegnare, 27
drawbridge, il ponte levatoio, 25
drawer, il cassettino, 3
dress, il vestito, 7

dresser, la toletta, 2
dressing room, il camerino, 19
drill, il trapano, 3
drink, bere, 27
drive, guidare, 27
drive-in, il servizio per le automobili, 13
driver's seat, il sedile del guidatore, 14
driveway, la strada privata, 8
drugstore, la farmacia, 8
drum, il tamburo, 19
dry, secco, 26
duck, l'anitra, 9
duckling, l'anatroccolo, 9
dull, non tagliente, 26
dungeon, il carcere sotterraneo, 25
dust, il polvere, 4
dustpan, la paletta della spazzatura, 3

eagle, l'aquila, 20
ear, l'orecchio, 11
earmuffs, il paraorecchie, 7
earring, l'orecchino, 7
Earth, la Terra, 23
easel, il cavalletto, 1
east, est, 32
easy, facile, 26
eat, mangiare, 27
eggs, le uova, 6
eight, otto, 31
eighteen, diciotto, 31
eighth, ottavo, 31
eighty, ottanta, 31
eighty-eight, ottantotto, 31
eighty-five, ottantacinque, 31
eighty-four, ottantaquattro, 31
eighty-nine, ottantanove, 31
eighty-one, ottantuno, 31
eighty-seven, ottantasette, 31
eighty-six, ottantasei, 31
eighty-three, ottantatrè, 31
eighty-two, ottantadue, 31
elbow, il gomito, 11
electric mixer, il miscelatore, 3
electric train, il trenino, 4
electrical outlet, la presa, 3
electrician, l'elettricista, 15
elephant, l'elefante, 20, 21
elevator, l'ascensore, 17
eleven, undici, 31
elf, l'elfo, 25
empty, vuoto, 26
engine, il motore, 14, 17
equator, l'equatore, 32
eraser (chalkboard), il cancellino, 1; (pencil), la gomma, 1
escalator, la scala mobile, 17
Europe, l'Europa, 32
examining table, la tavola da esaminare, 11
eyebrow, il sopracciglio, 11
eyes, gli occhi, 11

face, la faccia, 11
factory, la fabbrica, 8
factory worker, l'operaia, 15
fairy, la maga, 25
fall, cadere, 27
fall (season), l'autunno, 5
family tree, l'albero di famiglia, 29
fan (hand), il ventaglio, 4; (electric), il ventilatore, 5
far, lontano, 26
farm, la fattoria, 9
farmer, l'agricoltore, 9
fashion designer, la stilista, 15
fast, rapido, 26
fat, grasso, 26
father, il padre, 29
faucet, il rubinetto, 3
fault, la faglia, 32
feather, la piuma, 4
feathers, le piume, 20

fence, il recinto, 9
fender, il paraurti, 14
fern, la felce, 24
field, il campo, 24
fifteen, quindici, 31
fifth, quinto, 31
fifty, cinquanta, 31
fifty-eight, cinquantotto, 31
fifty-five, cinquantacinque, 31
fifty-four, cinquantaquattro, 31
fifty-nine, cinquantanove, 31
fifty-one, cinquantuno, 31
fifty-seven, cinquantasette, 31
fifty-six, cinquantasei, 31
fifty-three, cinquantatrè, 31
fifty-two, cinquantadue, 31
file, la lima, 3
file cabinet, lo schedario, 13
film, la pellicola, 21
fin, la pinna, 22
find, trovare, 27
finger, il dito, 11
fingernail, l'unghia, 12
fire, il fuoco, 24
fire engine, l'autopompa, 16
fire escape, la scala di sicurezza, 8
fire fighter, il pompiere, 15
fire hydrant, l'idrante, 8
fire station, la stazione dei pompieri, 8
fireplace, il focolare, 2
first, primo, 31
fish, il pesce, 1, 10
fisherman, il pescatore, 15
fishhook, l'amo, 22
fishing, la pesca, 24
fishing line, la lenza, 22
five, cinque, 31
fix, aggiustare, 27
flags, le bandiere, 17
flamingo, il fenicottero, 20
flashbulb, il riflettore, 21
flashlight, la lampadina tascabile, 3
flat tire, la gomma a terra, 14
flight attendant, l'assistente di volo, 17
flint, la selce, 24
flipper, la pinna, 22
floor, il pavimento, 2
florist, la fiorista, 15
flour, la farina, 3
flowerbed, l'aiuola, 5
flowers, i fiori, 5
flute, il flauto, 19
fly (insect), la mosca, 5; (verb), volare, 27
fly swatter, il chiappamosche, 5
fog, la nebbia, 5
food, il cibo, 6
food processor, il food processor, 3
foot, il piede, 11
football (game), il football americano, 18; (ball), la palla, 18
footprint, l'orma, 23
footstool, il posapiedi, 2
forehead, la fronte, 11
foreman, il capomastro, 15
forest, la foresta, 25
forge, la fornace, 25
fork, la forchetta, 10
forty, quaranta, 31
forty-eight, quarantotto, 31
forty-five, quarantacinque, 31
forty-four, quarantaquattro, 31
forty-nine, quarantanove, 31
forty-one, quarantuno, 31
forty-seven, quarantasette, 31
forty-six, quarantasei, 31
forty-three, quarantatrè, 31
forty-two, quarantadue, 31
fountain, la fontana, 8
four, quattro, 5, 31
fourteen, quattordici, 31
fourth, quarto, 31
fox, la volpe, 20
freckles, le lentiggini, 12

freezer, il congelatore, 3
french fries, le patatine fritte, 10
French horn, il cornetto, 19
frog, la rana, 9
frozen dinner, il pranzo surgelato, 6
fruit, le frutta, 6
fruit juice, il succo, 6
full, pieno, 26
fur, la pelliccia, 24

galaxy, la galassia, 23
game, il gioco, 4
garage, il garage, 14
garden hose, l'idrante, 5
gardener, il giardiniere, 15
garment bag, il sacco per abiti, 17
gas cap, il coperchio del serbatoio, 14
gas pump, la pompa della benzina, 14
gas station, la stazione di servizio, 14
gate, la porta, 17
giant, il gigante, 25
gift, il regalo, 10
gills, le branchie, 22
giraffe, la giraffa, 20
girl, la ragazza, 9
give, dare, 27
glacier, il ghiacciaio, 32
glass, il bicchiere, 10
glasses, gli occhiali, 7
globe, il globo, 1
gloves, i guanti, 7
glue, la colla, 1
go, andare, 27
go! avanti, 16
goat, la capra, 9
goggles, gli occhiali di protezione, 18
gold (color), dorato, 28; (metal), l'oro, 22
golf, il golf, 18
golf club, la mazza da golf, 18
good, buono, 26
goose, l'oca, 9
gorilla, il gorilla, 20
gosling, il papero, 9
grandfather, il nonno, 29
grandma, la nonna, 29
grandmother, la nonna, 29
grandpa, il nonno, 29
grapefruit, il pompelmo, 6
grapes, le uva, 6
grass, l'erba, 9
grasshopper, la cavalletta, 5
gray, grigio, 28
green, verde, 28
green beans, i fagiolini, 6
grocery store, la drogheria, 8
guitar, la chitarra, 19
gulf, il golfo, 32
gym shoes, le scarpe da tennis, 7
gymnastics, la ginnastica, 18

hair, i capelli, 12
hair dryer, l'asciugacapelli, 12
hair spray, lo spruzzo, 12
hairstylist, la parrucchiera, 12
half, metà, 31
ham, il prosciutto, 10
hamburger, la svizzera, 10
hammer, il martello, 3
hammock, l'amaca, 5
hand (clock), la lancetta, 1; (person), la mano, 11
hand brake, il freno a mano, 14
handkerchief, il fazzoletto, 7
handlebars, il manubrio di bicicletta, 14
handstand, la verticale, 21
hang glider, l'aliante, 16
hangar, l'aviorimessa, 17
hanger, l'attaccapanni, 2
happy, felice, 26
hard, duro, 26
harp, l'arpa, 19
hat, il cappello, 4, 7

hay, il fieno, 9
head, la testa, 11
headlight, il fanale, 14
headset, la cuffia, 17
headstand, la verticale sulla testa, 21
heavy, pesante, 26
helicopter, l'elicottero, 16
helm, l'elmo, 22
helmet, l'elmetto, 18
hen, la gallina, 9
high jump, il salto in alto, 18
hiking boots, gli scarponi, 7
hill, la collina, 9
hippopotamus, l'ippopotamo, 20
history, la storia, 24
hockey, l'hockey, 18
hole punch, la perforatrice per carta, 1
hood (clothing), il cappuccio, 7; (car), il cofano, 14
hoof, lo zoccolo, 20
hoop, il cerchio, 21
horns, le corna, 9, 20
horse, il cavallo, 9
horse racing, la corsa da cavalli, 18
horseback riding, l'equitazione, 18
horseshoe, il ferro di cavallo, 25
hospital, l'ospedale, 8
hot, caldo, 26
hot-air balloon, il pallone, 16
hotel, l'albergo, 8
house, la casa, 2
hubcap, il coprimozzo, 14
human history, la storia umana, 24
hump, la gobba, 20
hundred, cento, 31
hundred thousand, cento mila, 31
hunt, la caccia, 26
hunter, il cacciatore, 24
hurdles, la corsa a ostacoli, 18
hut, la capanna, 2
hypodermic needle, l'ago, 11

ice, il ghiaccio, 5
ice cream, il gelato, 10
ice cubes, i ghiacci, 3
iceberg, l'iceberg, 32
icecap, la calotta polare, 32
icicle, il ghiacciolo, 5
in front of, davanti, 26
Indian Ocean, l'Oceano Indiano, 32
ink pad, il tampone, 13
insect, l'insetto, 24
inside, indietro, 26
intersection, l'incrocio, 16
iron, il ferro da stiro, 3
ironing board, la tavola da stiro, 3
island, l'isola, 32

jack, il cricco, 14
jacket, la giacca, 7
jaguar, il giaguaro, 20
jail, il carcere, 8
jam, la marmellata, 10
jeans, i jeans, 7
jeep, il jeep, 16
jellyfish, la medusa, 22
jewel, il gioiello, 22
jeweler, il gioielliere, 15
jigsaw puzzle, il rompicapo, 4
jogging, il footing, 18
judge, il giudice, 15
juggle, fare giochi, 27
juggler, il giocoliere, 21
jump, saltare, 27
jump rope, la corda, 4
jungle, la giungla, 32
jungle gym, l'attrezzo ginnico, 8

kangaroo, il canguro, 20
ketchup, il ketchup, 10
kettle, il bollitore, 3
key, la chiave, 13

kick, dare un calcio, 27
kickstand, il cavalletto, 14
kid, il capretto, 9
kiln, la fornace, 24
king, il re, 25
kitchen, la cucina, 2, 3
kite, l'aquilone, 5
kitten, il gattino, 9
knee, il ginocchio, 11
knife, il coltello, 10
knight, il cavaliere, 25
knitting needles, i ferri da calza, 4
knot, il nodo, 13

lab coat, il camice, 23
label, l'etichetta, 13
laboratory, il laboratorio, 23
ladder, la scala a pioli, 23
lake, il lago, 32
lamb, l'agnello, 9
lamp, la lampada, 2
lance, la lancia, 25
landing capsule, la capsula spaziale, 23
landing gear, il carrello d'atterraggio, 17
large, grande, 26
laugh, ridere, 27
laundry, il bucato, 3
laundry detergent, il detersivo, 3
lawn mower, la falciatrice meccanica, 5
lawyer, l'avvocatessa, 15
leaf, la foglia, 5
leather, il cuoio, 24
left, sinistro, 26
leg, la gamba, 11
lemon, il limone, 6
leopard, il gattopardo, 20
leotard, la calzamaglia, 19
letter, la lettera, 13
letter carrier, il postino, 15
lettuce, la lattuga, 6
librarian, il bibliotecario, 15
light (color), chiaro, 26; (weight), leggero, 26
lightbulb, la lampadina, 4, 21
lighthouse, il faro, 16
lightning, il fulmine, 5
lime, il tiglio, 6
lion, il leone, 20, 21
lion tamer, il domatore dei leoni, 21
lips, le labbra, 11
lipstick, il rossetto, 12
listen (to), ascoltare, 27
living room, il salotto, 2
lizard, la lucertola, 20
lobster, l'aragosta, 22
lock, la serratura, 13
log, il ceppo, 5
long, lunghi, 12; lungo, 26
long jump, il salto in lungo, 18
look for, cercare, 27
loom, il telaio, 24
loudspeaker, l'altoparlante, 1
luggage compartment, il deposito bagagli, 17
lunar rover, la macchina lunare, 23
lunch, il pranzo, 10

magazines, le riviste, 11
magic wand, la bacchetta magica, 25
magician, il mago, 21
magnet, il magnete, 4
mail slot, il buco delle lettere, 13
mailbag, il sacco da posta, 13
mailbox, la cassetta postale, 13
make-believe, immaginato, 25
makeup, il trucco, 19
mammoth, il mammùt, 24
man, l'uomo, 9
mane, la criniera, 20
manhole cover, la bocca di accesso, 8
manicurist, la manicure, 12
map, la carta geografica, 1, 32
marbles, le palline di marmo, 4
mascara, la mascara, 12
mask, la maschera, 19, 22

master of ceremonies, il cerimoniere, 19
matches, i fiammiferi, 5
meals, i pasti, 10
meat, la carne, 6
mechanic, il meccanico, 14
medal, la medaglia, 18
medicine, la medicina, 11
medicine cabinet, l'armadietto farmaceutico, 2
medium, medio, 26
melon, il melone, 6
menu, il menù, 10
metal detector, il revelatore del metallo, 17
meteor shower, la pioggia dei meteori, 23
mice, i topi, 26
microphone, il microfono, 19
microscope, il microscopio, 23
microwave oven, il forno a microonda, 3
milk, il latte, 6
million, milione, 31
minstrel, il menestrello, 25
mirror, lo specchio, 2
mittens, i guanti a manopola, 7
moat, il fosso, 25
model, l'indossatrice, 15
mom, la mamma, 29
money, il denaro, 6
monkey, la scimmia, 20
moon, la luna, 23
moon rock, il cristallo di luna, 23
mop, la scopa di stracci, 3
mother, la madre, 29
motorboat, il motoscafo, 16
motorcycle, la motocicletta, 16
mountains, la montagna, 32
mouse, il topo, 9
mousse, il mousse, 12
mouth, la bocca, 11
movie projector, il proiettore, 4
movie theater, il cinema, 8
mud, il fango, 5
museum, il museo, 8
mushroom, il fungo, 10
music box, la scatola della musica, 4
mustache, i baffi, 12
mustard, la mostarda, 10

nail, il chiodo, 3
nail clippers, il tagliaunghie, 12
nail file, la limaiola, 12
nail polish, lo smalto, 12
napkin, il tovagliolo, 10
narrow, stretto, 26
navigator, il navigatore, 17
near, vicino, 26
nebula, la nebulosa, 23
necklace, la collana, 7
nest, il nido, 5
net, la rete, 18
new, nuovo, 26
newspaper, il giornale, 8
next to, vicino a, 26
night, la notte, 21
night table, il tavolo, 2
nine, nove, 31
nineteen, diciannove, 31
ninety, novanta, 31
ninety-eight, novantotto, 31
ninety-five, novantacinque, 31
ninety-four, novantaquattro, 31
ninety-nine, novantanove, 31
ninety-one, novantuno, 31
ninety-seven, novantasette, 31
ninety-six, novantasei, 31
ninety-three, novantatrè, 31
ninety-two, novantadue, 31
ninth, nono, 31
noodles, la pasta, 10
north, nord, 32
North America, l'America del Nord, 32
North Pole, il polo Nord, 32
northeast, nord-est, 32
northwest, nord-ovest, 32
nose, il naso, 11

notebook, il quaderno, 1
notepad, il blocco, 13
numbers, i numeri, 1, 31
nurse, l'infermiere, 11
nuts, le noci, 6

oar, il remo, 16
oasis, l'oasi, 32
ocean, l'oceano, 22
octagon, l'ottagono, 30
octopus, il polpo, 22
off, spento, 26
oil, l'olio, 14
old, vecchio, 26
omelet, la frittata, 10
on, acceso, 26
on top of, su, 26
one, uno, 31
onions, le cipolle, 6
open (adjective), aperto, 26; (verb), aprire, 27
optician, l'ottico, 15
orange (color), arancione, 28; (fruit), l'arancia, 6
orchestra, l'orchestra, 19
orchestra pit, la buca dell'orchestra, 19
ordinal numbers, i numeri ordinali, 31
ostrich, lo struzzo, 20
outside, fuori, 26
oval, l'ovale, 30
oven, il forno, 3
owl, il gufo, 20
oxygen tank, l'autorespiratore, 22

Pacific Ocean, l'Oceano Pacifico, 32
package, il pacco, 13
packing tape, il nastro d'imballaggio, 13
paint (verb), dipingere, 27; (noun), il colore, 1, 24
paintbrush, il pennello, 1
painter, il pittore, 15
pajamas, la pigiama, 7
pan, la padella, 3
panda, l'orso panda, 20
pants, i pantaloni, 7
paper, la carta, 1
paper clip, la graffa, 13
paper towels, l'asciugamani di carta, 3
parachute, il paracadute, 18
paramedic, l'assistente del medico, 15
park, il parco, 8
parking lot, il parcheggio, 8
parking meter, il parchimetro, 8
parrot, il pappagallo, 20
part, la scriminatura, 12
passenger, il passeggero, 17
passenger's seat, il sedile del passeggero, 14
passport, il passaporto, 17
patient, il paziente, 11
paw, la zampa, 20
peach, la pesca, 6
peacock, il pavone, 20
peanuts, le arachidi, 21
peas, i piselli, 6
pedal, il pedale, 14
pedicurist, la pedicure, 12
pen, la penna, 1
pencil, la matita, 1
pencil sharpener, il temperamatite, 1
penguin, il pinguino, 20
peninsula, la penisola, 32
people, la gente, 15
pepper, il pepe, 10
petal, il petalo, 5
pharmacist, la farmacista, 15
pharmacy, la farmacia, 8
phone booth, la cabina telefonica, 13
photo album, l'album di fotografie, 4
photograph, la foto, 4
photographer, il fotografo, 15
piano, il pianoforte, 19
picnic, il picnic, 9
picture, il quadro, 1
picture frame, la cornice, 4